h

The Greatness of the Shift

P.U.S.H. Don't Abort Your Purpose
Destiny Is Calling You into the
Greatness of the "SHIFT"

APOSTLE NADINE MANNING GLOBAL MINISTRIES INC.
www.apostlenadineglobal.com

Published by Kingdom Graphics Designo Inc. *(c) 10-18*

The Greatness of the Shift

Don't Abort Your Purpose Destiny is Calling You into "The Greatness of the SHIFT"

Copyright © June 06, 2017 by Apostle Dr. Nadine Manning

All rights reserved. No part of this book may be reproduced or transmitted in any form or by any means without written permission from the author.

ISBN 978-0-9898369-5-1

Printed in USA by Prophetic in Warfare Deliverance and Worship Tabernacle
in association with Kingdom Graphics Designo Inc.

Apostle Nadine Manning Global Ministries Inc.
P.O. Box 91, Millville New Jersey 08332.
apostlenadineglobal@gmail.com

Contents

The Greatness of the Shift 1
   Don't Abort Your Purpose 1
   Destiny is Calling You into 1
   "The Greatness of the SHIFT" 1
   Foreword 4
   Honorable Mention 6
   Prelude 11
   The GREATNESS of "THE SHIFT" 11

Chapter 1 22
Carrier of the "SHIFT" 22
   Divinely Chosen 27
   I Am Anointed for the Shift 31

Chapter 2 39
I Refuse to Die Here – I'm Ready to Shift 39
   Divine Guidance 42

Chapter 3 49
Faith in Action 49

Chapter 4 60
DREAM AGAIN TO SHIFT 60
   DNA of Destiny 68

Chapter 5 77
The Prophetic Announcement of Greatness 77
   Don't Be Afraid God is on Your Boat 82
The Suddenlies of God 90

Mega Blessings 94

Chapter 7 101
Get in the Shift...101
   Tipping Point 104
   Prophetic Reset 108
   The Threshing Floor Experience 114
Chapter 8 121
KINGDOM BUSTED TO P.U.S.H 121
Testimony of the Miraculous Birth of My Children 121
   The Power of Crying Out...126
Chapter 9 135
Kingdom Shifters..135
Chapter 10 150
Don't Abort Your Purpose Destiny Is Calling You 150
   A Promise is A Promise 152
   Expectation is the Breathing Ground for Miracles........158
Chapter 11 163
From Barrenness into Greatness 163
Chapter 12 178
Beware of Destiny Killers...178
   Don't Listen to Dream Killers 179
   Who Are You Eating With?...183
Chapter 13 187
The Glory is in Your Story..187

Foreword

I call her Prophetess, it is her divine name since 1997. When I met Apostle Dr. Nadine Manning, she was a freshman in Bible College and the Lord led me to her classroom, three days consistently, to announce her divine name from Heaven "*Prophetess.*" I was her senior in Bible College at the time, and we had to go through her classroom to the cafeteria for recess each evening.

Unbeknown to me, I learnt after that she was praying to abort her purpose and ultimate destiny as a Prophet to the nations because of those who misunderstood her and rejected her. Prophetess shared with me after with tears in her eyes that she was in a three (3) fast to abort her purpose because she felt as if most people hated her style of expression and radical worship style as well as the prophetic warnings and instructions she would give. She was also told by another senior in Bible College that she needed deliverance because of the prophetic warnings of repentance and transformation she gave in Chapel. Few months later these same warnings foretold came to pass. This made her question her calling and decided to do what the person recommended to get delivered.

She attempted to abort her purpose back then because of the pressure thinking to herself then this call is not from God. So, she went into prayer and fasting to ask God to deliver her from the gift she too was learning and developing in that area of the prophetic. But God in His infinite wisdom led me to go her classroom the exact three (3) days of her secretly praying and fasting to renounce the gift to just speak life to the gift inside of her. All I did was say, *"Hello Prophetess"* and walked away. I did that for three (3) days consecutively. Each day I went to her class she would look at me queer. On the final day she spoke up saying, *"why do you call me "Prophetess?"* My response to her with a smile was, *"I didn't call you "Prophetess" the Lord calls you "Prophetess."*

On the fourth (4) day I ask one of our ministers from our prayer group to give her a message on my behalf inviting her to our all-night prayer group service usually held on Fridays. This group was later established as the Remnant Ministries International Ministries, as we travelled all over Jamaica doing Prayer and Deliverance Crusades, all night prayer meetings, individual counselling and deliverance sessions, as well as revivals and conferences in various churches. Prophetess was a member of the Remnant Ministries until she migrated in 2003 and signs and wonders followed her Prophetic Ministry. She is very passionate about Prayer, Intercession and Worship and is an Anointed Spiritual Warfare Strategist.

This dedicated servant of God has fought many battles on many facets of life's spheres and has garnered a wealth of experience in praise, worship and spiritual warfare. Her testimonies of victory and triumphs are many. The wisdom gained in the processes of her life God has enabled her to shear with others to raise them up like Elijah raised up Elisha.

You will be truly blessed by reading this publication.

Reverend, Norman Lewin
Spiritual Father and Bishop
Kingdom Builders Open Bible
Spanish Town, Jamaica W.I.

Honorable Mention

First and foremost, I give all honor and glory to the Lord of Life, Savior of my soul Jesus Christ. I thank God for giving me a new life through His Son, Jesus Christ. The overwhelming grace and mercy of my Lord and Savior Jesus Christ, nothing good I've done to deserve this love has granted me through His mighty power the opportunity and divine ability to uncover my untapped potential through many painful trials and suffering. As a result of which I am thankful that out of my painful and unexpected life setbacks the Lord used it to catapult me into "The Greatness of the Shift". I have shared bits and pieces of my story in my first and second book, **"Awake to Your Destiny"** and **"I Am Anointed for This,"** available on Amazon.com. But this book gives a more complete focus and revelation on the challenges I had to overcome to give birth to my children and what looked like it was working against me was really preparing me to help others experience the **"Greatness of the Shift."**

Through the anointing on my life cultivated through the refining process of my fiery trials, the Lord has birthed out of me a multifaced global ministry hosting Global Conferences annually to impact lives and bring about a change. Conferences such as the **"Prophetic Destiny Shift"** Conference held annually in November and the March Conferences now titled the **"Holy Spirit Break**

Out" Engine Room Fire Conference designed to empower and bring deliverance to people who have travelled from out of state, as well as overseas from the United Kingdom, Canada and Jamaica to receive supernatural breakthroughs and experience Mega-Shifts perpetually in their lives.

Over 24 years in ministry, but the last (14) years has been the greatest testing and trails of my life noted in my first and second book and now this book exceed them all because it embodies my painful journey from *"Bareness into Greatness."* I've been teaching and preaching on the theme **"SHIFT"** for over seven (7) years and held yearly watch night services using the **"Shift"** as a theme, such as, **"Get into the Shift"**, **"Paradigm Shift"** and then four years ago we relaunched the November, **"Ingathering of God's Army Conference"** as the annual **"Prophetic Shift Conference."** Little did I know that the Lord was building a momentum for me to release this book titled *"The Greatness of the Shift"*, *Don't Abort Your Purpose Destiny is Calling You into "The Greatness of the Shift."* during this November 09th to 12th Prophetic Conference under the same theme, **"THE GREATNESS OF THE SHIFT."** This book is Volume 1 of the Birthing Process Series and I can't wait to see what's next for Volume 2 of the **"Greatness of the Shift"** will be continued at various levels, glory to God.

Honorable Mention is given to my children, who indeed was birthed out for Greatness. I thank God for being your mother in the natural and the spiritual and indeed you are carrier of **"The Greatness of the Shift"** and it is unstoppable and irrevocable that you are chosen to be **"Kingdom Shifters"** and **"Carriers of the Shift"** Anointing, glory to God.

Honorable Mention is also given to my Mother, Dorothy Nicholas who was their right through every painful moment of my late husband illness and after the birth f the triplets you came to help nurture them and see them transform to this period of their preteen life. Likewise, you were there when I needed help, along with my father, Oswald Nicholas taking care of the triplets for almost three (3) months in Jamaica until I gave birth to Joshua. Also want to give thanks to my sisters, Ingrid and Georgia Nicholas who assisted during that time. Not to mention my Aunt Erica Brown living in Florida who paid her way to Jamaica to help bring the triplet back to New Jersey after I had Joshua, thank you.

Honorable Mention to my Spiritual Father Reverend, Bishop Norman Lewin who wrote the Foreword for this book. He was integral in me not aborting my destiny why I can write Volume one (1) of **"The Greatness of the Shift."** You will be hearing about my ministry journey in volume two (2).

Honorable Mention to Apostle Dr, Bishop Richard A. McKenzie who inspired me since the day we divinely connected November 2014, to write the book that unfold the testimonies of my fiery trials leading to the miraculous birth of the Triplet, Aaron, Nathaniel and Abigail as well as the birth of Joshua suddenly. He spoke to me prophetically as well to write the book and hold nothing back.

Honorable Mention of Dr. Sheldon McKenzie who is an avid supporter of this ministry and when I relaunched the November Conferences as he Prophetic Shift Conference. Thank you for never missing a Shift Conference, even when he relocated from Washington D.C. to Oregon made willing sacrifice to divinely connect for **"The Shift."** Thank you for our encouragement as you also spoke prophetically to me as our Guest Speaker in 2016. Prophetic Shift Conference saying, *"Apostle write that book before someone else write it."* So here I am unleashing this epic and dynamic book, **"The Greatness of the Shift."**

Honorable mention to all my spiritual daughters and sons I mentored and training in spiritual warfare and intercession who prayed for me since our divine connection.

Honorable Mention to Bishop George and Reverend Beverly George from Peterborough, United Kingdom whom I have adopted as spiritual parent through the divine connection of Andrea and Ian Smith, who also prayers and support this ministry. Thank you all for your continued love, prayers and support.

Honorable Mention of Reverend Rohan and Minister Sonia Anderson who showed me unconditional love in the UK and prayed for me as well as spoke life to me during a very difficult transition in m life and ministry.

Honorable Mention to Pastor and First Lady Dawkins who has been their as encouragers and spiritual guidance for me since I gave my life to Christ. Thanks to Janette Barclay, First Lady Dawkins sister who has divinely connected to this ministry and my personal life as a watchman on the wall for over seventeen (17) years, thank you for your unconditional love and prayers.

Honorable mention to Dr. Susan James as well as Apostle David Trusty, stalwarts doing bidding through **"The Courts of Heaven"** on my behalf continually for me breakthrough since we divinely connected less than two (2) years ago.

Thanks to everyone who came into my life and did your part to challenge me, push me and encourage me to discover and unlock the greatness within me.

Yours in Christ,

Apostle Dr. Nadine Manning
Prophetic Destiny Pusher and
Apostolic Voice to the Nations

Prelude

The GREATNESS of "THE SHIFT"

Now the LORD had said to Abram: "Get out of your country, from your family and from your father's house, to a land that I will show you. [2] I will make you a great nation; I will bless you and make your name great; And you shall be a blessing. [3] I will bless those who bless you, And I will curse him who curses you; And in you all the families of the earth shall be blessed" [Genesis 12:1-3 NKJV].

Genesis Chapter 12 prophetically announces the Divine Revelation and mystery of the **"The Greatness of the "SHIFT."** Through the life of Abraham God has set the tone from history throughout all generations that will change our Destiny into one without limitations called Greatness.

- **Greatness** comes from the word '**Great**' meaning: Extraordinary, not normal or average, worthy of honor, big, well known or matchless

- **Greatness** also means remarkable in magnitude, degree, or effectiveness.

Therefore, if **"Greatness"** means extraordinary, above average, remarkable in magnitude or size then the Lord is saying, get ready for expansion and enlargement of territory in Him. Get ready for promotion and increase in every area of your life.

> ***"You will enlarge the nation of Israel, and its people will rejoice. They will rejoice before you as people rejoice at the harvest and like warriors dividing the plunder"*** [Isaiah 9:3].

This is your season of joy and laughter, not mourning or sorrow, for you shall break forth on the right and left. You will see the manifestation of all that you have been praying for. This is your harvest season and your season of joy over your enemies.

> ***"Enlarge the place of thy tent, and let them stretch forth the curtains of thine habitations: spare not, lengthen thy cords, and strengthen thy stakes; 3 For thou shalt break forth on the right***

hand and on the left; and thy seed shall inherit the Gentiles, and make the desolate cities to be inhabited" [Isaiah 54:2].

- **Shift** means Change, it means moving from one place to the next.

It's time to move forward. Forgetting the former things and behold the new things the Lord has set forth. Its time to rebuild and reposition. The Lord is shifting out the old and preparing you for the new. For those in ministry that has suffered stagnation or loss and periods of setbacks you will build, and the people shall come. You will build, and the people shall follow. Whatever your lamentation, and seeking after God tirelessly for change, He has heard your cry and says, *"I am opening a door no man can shut."* Get ready for the new things and open door that no man can shut.

> *"Remember ye not the former things, neither consider the things of old. 19 Behold, I will do a new thing; now it shall spring forth; shall ye not know it? I will even make a way in the wilderness, and rivers in the desert"* [Isaiah 43:18-19].

> *"See, I have placed before you an open door, which no one can shut. For you have only a little strength, yet you have kept My word and have not denied My name"*
> [Revelation 3:8].

He told Abraham, to **"Get out of your country, from your family and from your father's house, to a land that I will show you."** The blessings were already established by God in a place called "There." The blessings were already there, all Abraham had to do was get up and pursue it, go after it. God has chosen you to experience the **"Greatness of the Shift"** like Abraham, but you must be willing to get up and go. You need to understand that your shift into greater lies in your obedience. Like Abraham you must trust God when he speaks. Abraham was called to experience **"The Greatness of the Shift"** and to set the precedence for us to possess and walk into our blessings through Jesus Christ. All we need to do initially is believe in our Lord Jesus Christ, who died and rose again, so we might be saved. It is through Jesus Christ we have access by faith into **"The Greatness of the Shift."**

"Therefore, having been justified by faith, [a]we have peace with God through our Lord Jesus Christ, 2 through whom also we have access by faith into this grace in which we stand" [Romans 5:1-2].

"Therefore, know that only those who are of faith are sons of Abraham. 8 And the Scripture, foreseeing that God would justify the Gentiles by faith, preached the gospel to Abraham beforehand, saying, "In you all the nations shall be blessed." 9 So then those who are of faith are blessed with believing Abraham" [Gelation 3:7-9].

You have **"Royal Access, It's Your Inheritance"** to the same promises and blessings given to Abraham by the Lord. Those who have faith and walk by faith [in obedience] are the real children of Abraham. It is a comforting promise and a great inheritance for all believers in every age and from every nation to share Abraham's blessing.

"The purpose was that the blessing of Abraham would come

to the Gentiles by Christ Jesus, so that we could receive the promised Spirit through faith [Galatians 3:14].

God spoke with Abraham to get ***'Ready, Set and Go'*** into **"The Greatness of the Shift."** Without hesitation, Abraham believed in God and His Prophetic Promises and acted upon it. Even though, they were not made fully evident until centuries later when Jesus died on the cross, that what God promised Abraham was answered in faith. Jesus Christ surrendered his life to his father's will, because of the redemptive plan to save mankind. Even during the greatest trial of Abraham life, when God ask him to sacrifice his son Isaac, Abraham took God at his word. **"The Greatness of the SHIFT"** requires you to take God at His word. Abraham was a Pioneer of Greatness, making him a Carrier of the Shift. As a pioneer or carrier of the Shift, his obedience breaks all demonic barriers or cycles that could possible stand in our way of entering in **"The Greatness of the Shift."** Better yet, what Christ did on the cross for us breaks all demonic barriers and cycles:

"And it shall come to pass in that day, that his burden shall be taken away from off thy shoulder, and his yoke from off thy neck, and the yoke shall be destroyed because of the anointing" [Isaiah 10:27].

The blessings the Lord has for us **"It's Already There"** but we must go after it. The blessings God has for you pushes you and propels you to go after it. You must be willing to make the sacrifices to step out of your comfort zone and walk by faith into the unknown.

- **Greatness means: significant, prominent, renown. It is a position power, success and respect.**

When God calls you into a covenant of blessings it is inevitable, irrevocable and you are **"Destined to Win."** The blessings or Prophetic Promises are already established by God and ultimately positions you to be blessed and others will be blessed. **"The Greatness of the Shift"** therefore establish you, it propels you and makes you win. **The Greatness of "THE SHIFT"** is marked by a Prophetic Promise from God. A Prophetic Promise is a Divine Promise from God. God's Prophetic Promise over your life is irrevocable and unstoppable. The promise to the believers according to God's word in Deuteronomy 7:14 says, ***"You shall be blessed above all peoples. There shall not be male or female barren among you nor among your livestock."***

God's promise to you is that, you shall come forth into your breakthrough. Everything that concerns you that seems barren and unfruitful God specializes in it. Our great and Almighty God will cause the barren places to spring forth. You will give birth and manifest fruitfulness. You will also realize as you go through the birthing process everything that you touch shall spring up and shall become fruitful.

The Greatness of "THE SHIFT" is designed and orchestrated by God for **"Birthing Your Prophetic Destiny."** When things seem to be breaking down or it appears by life trials that things are falling apart in your life that's a Divine Indicator that God is getting ready to build you up to a whole new dimension. In this new dimension is a 'GREATER REALM OF GLORY' where you will no longer struggle but you will begin to soar. **'Soar,"** indicating that you are mature enough and well equipped to handle certain challenges that overwhelmed you in your last season, which the Lord will use to catapult you into your **"Due Season."** You will soar, you will mount up with wings as the eagle.

> *"But those who trust in the Lord will find new strength.*
> *They will soar high on wings like eagles.*
> *They will run and not grow weary.*
> *They will walk and not faint"*
> [Isaiah 40:31].

Because, in your **"Due Season"** of new things or new beginning, the Lord will conquer these dark forces and strongholds shifting your level of thinking to accelerate you into your Prophetic Destiny. This can only be described as **"The Greatness of "THE SHIFT."**

"The Greatness of the Shift" is experienced by a people who refuse to die. It is experienced by people who are convinced and confident that God is a Promise Keeper and He is faithful to fulfill and bring to pass that which He purposed to do for then that trust Him and hope in His word.

Exodus 20:2 declares, ***"I am the Lord your God, who brought you out of the land of Egypt, out of the house of bondage."*** You will experience **"The Greatness of "THE SHIFT"** as the Lord makes all things new to you just as when He delivered from the bondage of Satan and drew you to Himself to be His people. **"The Greatness of "THE SHIFT"** is the beginning of a new life.

Every believer who accepted Jesus Christ as their Lord and Savior has within them the power and creative ability to possess 'GREATNESS.'
I prophecy over your life that "You are Destined for Greatness." I prophecy to you that you are being positioned for ***"The Greatness of the Shift"***

> 1 Peter 2:9, declares, ***"But you are a chosen generation, a royal priesthood, a holy nation, His own special people, that you may proclaim the praises of Him who called you out of darkness into His marvelous light."***

The Divine Power of the Holy Spirit has given us the ability and strength to unlock the greatness within us. We cannot do that if we give up or turn back from the faith we truly confess in our Lord and Savior Jesus Christ. This is a now word to us as God is preparing us for **"The Greatness of the Shift"** globally. Like Gideon, you will have supernatural encounters that will change your life and make all things new. **"The Greatness of The Shift"** is the beginning of a new life. **"The Greatness of the**

SHIFT" will manifest, when you find yourself at the crossroads of a situation where you can't go backwards, and the only way forward is to breakthrough that dark place or Red Sea and the only thing you must stand on is **"The Prophetic Promise."**

- What has the Lord placed within you as a great idea for business, a talent to financially help yourself?
- What is that dream or vision the Lord gave you for your personal life, marriage, children or ministry?

"I prophecy to you that this is your divine moment to dream again.

I decree and declare: -

- *May the chapters of this book, enlarge your capacity to hold more of what God has in store for you.*
- *May the chapters of this book ignite and restore the fire in you.*
- *May your dreams come alive again.*
- *May your visions be restored and activated as you are inspired and empowered through the pages of this book.*
- *May you experience a supernatural translation and divine visitation as you read, propelling you to enter* **"The Greatness of the Shift."**

Chapter 1

Carrier of the "SHIFT"

A **Carrier of the "SHIFT"** is one chosen by God to bring about a change in the earth. They carry within their loins the anointing to **"SHIFT"** men and women into alignment to God's Divine Plan. These chosen **"Carriers of the Shift"** are **"Kingdom Shifters"** with their own personal encounter and the revelatory knowledge embedded in the DNA of their Destiny concerning the *Mystery of the Shift* given to them by the Holy Spirit. The Lord is refining and preparing a people who are willing to separate themselves as a Kingdom of Priest. This is a remnant who desire to walk in holiness before the Lord and represent Him as **"Carriers of the Shift."**

> *"And he shewed me Joshua the high priest standing before the angel of the Lord, and Satan standing at his right hand to resist him. 2 And the Lord said*

unto Satan, The Lord rebuke thee, O Satan; even the Lord that hath chosen Jerusalem rebuke thee: is not this a brand plucked out of the fire? 3 Now Joshua was clothed with filthy garments and stood before the angel. 4 And he answered and spake unto those that stood before him, saying, Take away the filthy garments from him. And unto him he said, Behold, I have caused thine iniquity to pass from thee, and I will clothe thee with change of raiment. 5 And I said, let them set a fair mitre upon his head. So, they set a fair mitre upon his head, and clothed him with garments. And the angel of the Lord stood by. 6 And the angel of the Lord protested unto Joshua, saying, 7 Thus saith the Lord of hosts; If thou wilt walk in my ways, and if thou wilt keep my charge, then thou shalt also judge my house, and shalt also keep my courts, and I will give thee places to walk among these that stand by. 8 Hear now, O Joshua the high priest, thou, and thy fellows that sit before thee: for they are men wondered at: for, behold, I will bring forth my servant the BRANCH. 9 For behold the stone

that I have laid before Joshua; upon one stone shall be seven eyes: behold, I will engrave the graving thereof, saith the Lord of hosts, and I will remove the iniquity of that land in one day. 10 In that day, saith the Lord of hosts, shall ye call every man his neighbour under the vine and under the fig tree" [Zechariah 3:1-10].

Joshua was Israel high priest when the remnant returned to rebuild the temple of Jerusalem. Joshua the high priest was one divinely chosen by God to represent the nations as he stands on trial before God. Joshua was high priest at the time when the Jews initially returned from Babylonian captivity. The posture of the priest is to stand before the Lord at the altar for his sins and the sins of the people. Zechariah 1:1-4 depicts Joshua the high priest posture as one being on trial before the Lord and Satan the accuser or adversary also presented himself.

The ministering angels were called by the Angel of the Lord to cleanse Joshua. This was a symbolic cleansing of God's people as verse 4b says, **"Take away the filthy garments."** In verse 1, Satan stands on the right hand of the angel of the Lord to suggest or imply that that the Jews might as well abandon all their hopes of rebuilding the temple and worshiping God, because their priests were corrupt and could not offer proper sacrifices to God. Furthermore, it is implied in the verses above that, they might as well stop the reconstruction of the temple, which could never be used in a way that would honor God because of the sinful practices.

The promise in Zechariah 3:9 is that God ***"will remove the iniquity of that land."*** Just as Joshua here is representing the entire land, with a change of raiment, his garments or beautiful robe was symbolic for the assignment as high priest. Likewise, there is a special or peculiar anointing released in this end time for the **"Carriers of the Shift."** Their assignments will be unique. The assignments will also be specific based on the individual prophetic instructions given to each person divinely chosen by God. The priests wore their robes on special occasions chosen for his priestly duty. Likewise, **"Carriers of the Shift"** has a peculiar anointing for special assignments and occasions the Lord has assigned them to greatly impact and transform nations, their communities, market place for some, ministry and family. They operate solely by the Holy Spirit divine guidance and divine instructions for their Kingdom Destiny. Whatever they were chosen to do was already predestined like Jeremiah and embedded in their DNA of Destiny [Jeremiah 1:5].

> *"Before I formed thee in the belly, I knew thee; and before thou camest forth out of the womb I sanctified thee, and I ordained thee a prophet unto the nations."*

Joshua's transformation in new raiment also, foreshadows the work of Christ, and of the righteousness that he gives to all who believe on him, which is beautiful in the eyes of God. Jesus was the great High Priest, and like Joshua, he represented the kingdom of Israel, which was a kingdom of priests. All the Lord is asking of you is to be open, willing and gracefully broken before Him. Repentance must precede this new wave of Glory released for the **"Greatness of the Shift"**

Although in Zechariah 1:1-10 the full fulfillment of this prophecy is still in the future, when Satan is finally rebuked and silenced, the people were sufficiently encouraged to get on with the construction of the temple. Prophetically speaking we are in the season where God sees the heart of those crying out for change who desires to build the Kingdom of

God. As a result of which the Lord will purify a remnant to become **"Carriers of the Shift"** and He will rebuke and silence the enemy on your behalf.

Divinely Chosen

In my first book, **"Awake to Your Destiny"** chapter 7 entitled **"I Am Chosen"** will give explicit details on how we're chosen and our divine access. But here is an excerpt on the definition and revelation flowing from that chapter.

- **Chosen means**: You have been selected, or preferred.
- Chosen is defined by scriptural reference as you have been predestined.
- You have been appointed by God to walk like Him and talk like Him. He gave a command saying,

> *"Let us make man into our image, after our likeness: and let them have dominion over the fish of the sea, and over the fowl of the air, and over the cattle, and over all the earth, and over every creeping*

thing that creepeth upon the earth" (Genesis 1:26).

God wanted a replica of Himself in the earth. He originally made man from what had no life (dust) and said now live. God breathe the breath of His life into man and said now think like me. God says to you today, *"I have given you the mind of Christ, the wisdom and the counsel of God; The authority invested in Me has been given to you."*

"Carriers of the Shift" are divinely chosen by the Lord. A great example to start with to biblically describe a **"Carrier of the Shift"** is seen from the Book of Joshua. Joshua the high priest mention earlier is different from the one mentioned in the Bok of Joshua. Moses was the predecessor of Joshua. Joshua was a **"Kingdom Shifter"** whom God called specifically for an assignment after Moses died. But Joshua Chapter 1 began where Deuteronomy ends and clearly outline the shift that was taking place after Moses died. This Kingdom Assignment given to Joshua was for him to pick up from where Moses ended and that was to take the people prepared and ready to **"SHIFT"** into the promise. When Joshua received this assignment, it was a time when it seemed like everything was at a standstill, Moses being dead.

When things seem dead, or as if you are at a dead end, it's a sign or indication of a **'New Thing or New Beginning'** don't panic, and fear not.

> *I prophetically announce to you that if you find yourself in this position, it is a pivotal point or into a* **"New Beginning."** *God shall carry you into a new thing and what you experience you will not be able to keep it to yourself. I decree and declare that you shall become a* **"Carrier of the Shift"** *to propel or lead others into the fullness of their blessings and destiny.*

Throughout the Bible from Genesis to Revelation it always seems like God announces something new, by revelation when things are very dark, hopeless or when it seems like there is no way out. Joshua was chosen by God to complete a Divine Assignment after the death of Moses, in Joshua 1:1-3.

"Now after the death of Moses the servant of the Lord it came to

pass, that the Lord spake unto Joshua the son of Nun, Moses' minister, saying, ² Moses my servant is dead; now therefore arise, go over this Jordan, thou, and all this people, unto the land which I do give to them, even to the children of Israel" [KJV].

"After the death of Moses, the Lord's servant, the Lord spoke to Joshua son of Nun, Moses' assistant. He said, ² "Moses my servant is dead. Therefore, the time has come for you to lead these people, the Israelites, across the Jordan River into the land I am giving them" [NLT].

As the book of Joshua opens it revealed that the Israelites were camped by the east of the Jordan River at the edge of the Promise Land as they completed their mourning period for Moses, who had just died [Deuteronomy 34:7-8]. Thirty-nine (39) years had passed since they received God's law. The Israelites had an opportunity to enter the Promise Land, but they failed to trust God to give them victory. Because of this, the older generation were not allowed to enter the land. Instead, God made them wander in the wilderness until the disobedient generation all died.

During that time of wandering they also taught a new generation to obey God's laws so that they might enter the Promise Land (Canaan Land). God is seeking a remnant to bring about the change in the earth. The **"Greatness of the Shift"** is all about entering the Prophetic Promise God has predestinated for your life. **"The Greatness of the Shift"** cannot be activated or manifested without your participation. As revealed from the Israelites history the older generation died because of disobedience. God desires to raise up a **"New Breed,"** a new generation to not only experience the supernatural encounter of **"The Greatness of the Shift"** but also to become **"Carriers of the Shift."**

I Am Anointed for the Shift

> *"The Spirit of the Lord God is upon me; because the Lord hath anointed me to preach good tidings unto the meek; he hath sent me to bind up the brokenhearted, to proclaim liberty to the captives, and the opening of the prison to them that are bound;*

2 To proclaim the acceptable year of the Lord, and the day of vengeance of our God; to comfort all that mourn; 3 To appoint unto them that mourn in Zion, to give unto them beauty for ashes, the oil of joy for mourning, the garment of praise for the spirit of heaviness; that they might be called trees of righteousness, the planting of the Lord, that he might be glorified. 4 And they shall build the old wastes, they shall raise up the former desolations, and they shall repair the waste cities, the desolations of many generations. 5 And strangers shall stand and feed your flocks, and the sons of the alien shall be your plowmen and your vinedressers. 6 But ye shall be named the Priests of the Lord: men shall call you the Ministers of our God: ye shall eat the riches of the Gentiles, and in their glory shall ye boast yourselves. 7 For your shame ye shall have double; and for confusion they shall rejoice in their portion: therefore in their land they shall possess the double" [Isaiah 61:1-7].

Joshua was chosen to be a **"Carrier of the Shift"** and God gave him the assurance that I will anoint you for the shift. When God anoints you for the shift, He guarantees by the power of the Holy Spirit within you that you will not fail, and He releases in the DNA of your Destiny the **"Power to Conquer and WIN."**

> *"I promise you what I promised Moses: 'Wherever you set foot, you will be on land I have given you— ⁴ from the Negev wilderness in the south to the Lebanon mountains in the north, from the Euphrates River in the east to the Mediterranean Sea[a] in the west, including all the land of the Hittites.' ⁵ No one will be able to stand against you as long as you live. For I will be with you as I was with Moses. I will not fail you or abandon you"* [Joshua 1:3-5].

The Lord told Joshua, **"I promise you what I promise Moses."** The Lord promised Joshua that He will not leave Him, **"I will be with you as I was with Moses, I will not fail you or abandon you."** Joshua was one of the only two living eyewitnesses to the Egyptian plagues and Israel Exodus from Egypt. He was

Moses personal assistant, and only he and Caleb showed complete confidence that God would help them conquer the land. God will not transfer or place a mantle upon someone who have not passed the test. You must have complete confidence in the promise or kingdom assignment given to you even when things seem impossible or appears dim in the natural.

    A **"Carrier of the Shift"** is someone not only marked or **"Destined for Greatness"** but carries within their lions the power and the authority to the unlocking of greatness within themselves and then for others. Joshua's preparation to become a **"Carrier of the Shift"** began during the rigorous test of the Israelites faith when God took them through the wilderness to prove what was in their heart.

    You must be able to endure to the end your hard-pressed tests or trials to experience **"The Greatness of the Shift"** before God can appoint you to become a **"Carrier of the Shift."** Joshua demonstrated those qualities. Are you ready to arise and conquer? Not every person is called to conquer nations but every day you will be faced with tough situations, difficult people, temptations or assignments that you must arise and conquer. The Lord promises that He will not abandon or fail you. **"Carriers of the Shift"** are

"Empowered to Go" but they must remain strong and courageous to experience **"The Greatness of the Shift"** from Glory to Glory. **"Carriers of the Shift"** must remain steadfast and focus on the promise, [Joshua 1:6-8].

> *"Be strong and courageous, for you are the one who will lead these people to possess all the land I swore to their ancestors I would give them. ⁷ Be strong and very courageous. Be careful to obey all the instructions Moses gave you. Do not deviate from them, turning either to the right or to the left. Then you will be successful in everything you do."*

If you desire to experience **"The Greatness of the Shift"** and ultimately become a **"Carrier of the Shift"** you cannot deviate from the purpose to which you have been assigned regardless of the challenges. As a **"Carrier of the Shift"** you will not fail ***"You Will Win."***

The Strategy to Becoming a Carrier of the Shift is:

- To be strong and courageous because the task ahead will not be easy.

- Obey God's Word, and constantly meditate upon it.
- Follow God's His divine instruction or direction given to you.

"The Greatness of the Shift" indicates that our life is being controlled by God and that is the underlying prerequisites to become a **"Carrier of the Shift."** It means that your life is already yielded and humbly submitted to the Lord. When you have experienced the **"Greatness of the Shift"** it means that you have succeeded in God's eyes because you live by His word despite the afflictions, hard trials and life uncertainties.

Be reminded again that, God wanted a replica of Himself in the earth. He originally made man from what had no life (dust) and said now live. God breathe the breath of His life into man and said now think like me. God says to you today, *"I have given you the mind of Christ, the wisdom and the counsel of God; the authority invested in Me is given to you to be a Carrier of the "SHIFT."* In my first book, **"Awake to Your Destiny," Volume 1 – "The Mind of Christ"** Chapter 7, "I Am Chosen" I shared that: -

"Then God blessed them and said, "Be fruitful and multiply. Fill the earth and govern it. Reign over the fish in the sea, the birds in the sky, and all the animals that scurry along the ground." 29 Then God said, "Look! I have given you every seed-bearing plant throughout the earth and all the fruit trees for your food. 30 And I have given every green plant as food for all the wild animals, the birds in the sky, and the small animals that scurry along the ground—everything that has life." And that is what happened" (Genesis 1:28-30).

God needed someone to manage the things He established in the earth, to teach and instruct others to take dominion over them and over everything God placed on the earth. It was Satan that beguiled Eve who then enticed Adam to eat the forbidden fruit that brought sin upon the earth. But God in His grace and mercy sent to us salvation through the shed blood of Jesus Christ. His goal was to redeem man so that they be awaken from dead works of the flesh and walk as children of light and manifest **"The Greatness of the Shift."**

When God called Abram into **"The Greatness of the Shift"** He moved out in faith from Ur to Haran and then to Canaan. God then established a covenant with Abram, revealing to him that he would be the pioneer and of a great nation. Not only would this nation be blessed, God said, but the other nations of the earth would be blessed through Abram's descendants. Israel, the nation that would come from Abram, was to follow God and influence those with whom it came in contact. Through Abram's family tree, Jesus Christ was born to save humanity. Through Christ, we can have a personal relationship with God and be blessed beyond measure.

    "The Greatness of the Shift" is announcing that the blessing of the Lord that salvation gives you will change your life completely. It turns your life around miraculously, it gives you the supernatural ability to do things that was impossible to do natural means. The mystery of the **"Shift"** is based on faith and the power of God at work in your life. The Lord has already imparted through your spiritual DNA the power and ability to unlock the greatness within you. **"The Greatness of the Shift"** pushes you from feeling or living ordinary to extraordinary. It takes you into a realm where you will live from victory to victory. All you need to do is position yourself and be ready to shift.

Chapter 2

I Refuse to Die Here – I'm Ready to Shift

"The Greatness of the Shift" is experienced by a people who refuse to die. There are greater things God has in store for you. God has greater things in store for us as a people. The four lepers at the gate made up in their minds to **"P.U.S.H.** [Persevere - Until - the SHIFT – Happens]. The four lepers at the gate in 2 Kings 7:3-4 made a Declaration of Faith that **"I Won't Die Here."**

> *"Now there were four leprous men at the entrance of the gate; and they said to one another, "Why are we sitting here until we die? 4 If we say, 'We will enter the city,' the famine is in the city, and we shall die there. And if we sit here, we die also. Now therefore, come, let us surrender to the army of the Syrians. If they keep us alive, we*

shall live; and if they kill us, we shall only die."

When you are leprous, or you have been diagnosed with a disease called leprosy you are not allowed to be around people that are considered clean. Anyone that has this disease becomes isolated. You are considered rejected, your condition brands you as unclean and so you must stay away from those considered clean, so they are not contaminated. Leprosy goes deep into your flesh and large soars grow out. As leprosy gets deeper it grows all over your body. The leprous man or woman is always suffering from pain constantly.

You may not be leprous physically like these men, but you may be facing excruciating circumstances or challenges that seem unbearable or unending. Moreover, your painful circumstances may have made you feel like a cast away, abandoned or rejected. Not that you want to be, but those you think would understand your pain, or be there during those devastating moments or transitioning period in your life may have given up on you. They may have been there for a while but when they realize that your condition is growing worse or graven rather than better, they pull away. I've walked through this dark period myself, several times. In fact, those who turned their backs on you, you were there for them during their suffering, testing or trial. You prayed for them, as well as fast on their behalf until they breakthrough and then suddenly you are at a crossroads in your life and the love, kindness and favors you expect from them is not reciprocated. Now that's painful to accept especially when you see them as a friend or confidant. God is rerouting you from the detours of miscalculated decisions and direction for **"The Greatness of the Shift"** into your ultimate purpose and destiny.

The four Lepers at the gate in the Book of 2 Kings chapter 7 were not allowed to enter the city, and if anyone came near them, they must cry out, *"unclean, unclean"* So everyone knew they had leprosy. Can you imagine everyone knows your issue, but you also must keep on confessing your condition that you are hopeless and in addition to that no one wants to be connected to you. Maybe in the work place, someone treats you as an outcast possibly because of your faith. It's possible that your life test or trial is not the case of a contagious disease, but rather an excellent spirit and work ethics that has made others feel uncomfortable and some to the point of jealous has decided to create false witness against you.

Your case maybe because you are gifted or talented like David or Joseph and it has stirred jealousy among those who feel intimidated by the uniqueness of the anointing you carry and the purpose to which you have been called by God. God hates the feet of those who are swift to do evil and this deliberate and malicious act by others to create mischief and provoke others to hate you.

> *"I decree and declare that a demand is being placed on Heaven and the Lord shall vindicate you by sending an angel to defeat your enemies in Jesus name, Amen." "I decree and declare that the Lord will use your fiery tests and trials to push you into the unlocking of* **"The Greatness of the Shift"** *for your breakthrough, blessings, miracles and your ultimate destiny."*

Divine Guidance

As mentioned in the introductory chapter of this divinely ordained book, **The Greatness of "THE SHIFT"** is marked by a **Prophetic**

Promise from God. A **Prophetic Promise is a Divine Promise** from God. God's Prophetic [Divine] Promise over your life is irrevocable and unstoppable. **"The Greatness of the Shift"** is released by God's Divine Hand. Everything about God is Divine, therefore, *"The Greatness of the Shift"* cannot be activated without **Divine Guidance.** Psalm 32:8 declares, *"I will instruct you and teach you in the way you should go, I will guide you with mine eyes*.

"Divine Guidance" refers to words or spiritual revelation inspired by the Holy Spirit, received by prophets with instructions or to point others in a specific direction. It can be words directly sent to you directly from God for yourself. Where there's ignorance, crime, sin can be rampant. Our standard morals that govern how we live depends on the knowledge of God, but it also depends on us hearing and obeying God's word. What we fail to understand is the worldly standards has filtered into our churches and faith base community due to a lack of faith and living by God's holy word.

For a nation to thrive and as individuals for us to function well, we must obey and follow God's ways and rules. This is done through proper guidance in God's word. Proper foundation in God's word is the landmark for any great move or outpouring of Gods Divine provision or release for your breakthrough. Divine Guidance or instructions is generally announced or proclaimed as a Great Shift through an Apostolic or Prophetic Voice. Divine Guidance for example is when God sent a prophetic word through the prophet Elisha in 2 Kings 7:1 saying: -

"Then Elisha said, "Hear the word of the LORD. Thus, says the LORD: 'Tomorrow about this time a seah of fine flour shall be sold for a shekel, and two seahs of barley for a shekel, at the gate of Samaria."

A Divine [Prophetic] Promise from the Lord when released you must accept it by faith. When the Prophet spoke the words to the people already suffering from hunger pains, emptiness, barrenness and poverty stricken, an officer of the King on whose hand the king leaned spoke death to the promise.

"So, an officer on whose hand the king leaned answered the man of God and said, "Look, if the LORD would make windows in heaven, could this thing be?" [2 Kings 7:2].

Doubt is the absence of faith. The King's Officer on whose hand the King leaned doubted **"The Greatness of this Shift."** The essence of his action is that, Elisha prophesied deliverance and the King's officer said it couldn't happen, his hope was gone. There are people filled with negative influence who will discourage you right at the brink of your breakthrough because they have lost sight of their own dreams and visions and refuse to move forward from dead issues because they have lost sight of their own visions and dreams. Now the enemy uses them to contaminate you for you to abort the promise. Don't miss this Divine Shift to *"Unlocking the Greatness Within you to Leap into Your Destiny"* because of doubters. Moreover, be very careful who you are sharing your personal desires, dreams and visions with. Don't be like the King's Officer who refuse to accept **"Divine Guidance"** for **"The Greatness of the Shift."** Proverbs 29:18 says,

> ***"When people do not accept Divine Guidance, they run wild. But those who obeys the law is joyful."***

Don't miss this Supernatural Shift from the Lord because of what others are saying and doing contrary to the Word of the Lord.

Be careful who you are open to when you are at a very vulnerable place and time in your life! Ask God to give you greater discernment because the enemy is very subtle. Our circumstances maybe the same but we don't have to die in it. We must align ourselves with people of like mind. A Faith Walker set of people with **"I refuse to die here, I'm Ready To SHIFT"** mentality. Elisha brought forth a word of Prophetic Release that **"This time tomorrow"** there shall be Divine Supplies, there will be Divine Provision. Elisha spoke to the people that there will be divine supplies, there will be Divine Provision, when there was scarcely anything to eat besides bird feces was for sale.

Elisha brought forth a Prophetic Revelation with Divine Instructions and Guidance in a time when women were killing their babies and eating their flesh that, **"Tomorrow about this time a seah of fine flour shall be sold for a shekel, and two seahs of barley for a shekel, at the gate of Samaria."** This Prophetic revelation was an indication that God was about to move on the people's behalf. God was about to show up in that dark place. God is saying *"Listen and Live and Be Ready to Shift."* So, they said among themselves, why should we **"sit here waiting to die."** They decided to take a Leap of Faith, saying "We will starve if we stay here, but with famine in the city, we will starve if we go back there" [2 Kings 7:4].

Step out by faith into the **"Greatness of the Shift."** With this Prophetic Announcement from the Prophet Elijah, the four lepers at the gate could no longer be content in their mess. They were no longer content in their dead state. They were ready to arise and activate what they felt in their spirit, that a **"Shift"** [change] is coming. They didn't know how or when in the natural, but in their spirit and heart they knew it was **"Time to Shift."** The word of the Lord was specific that food will be restored and at a very fair cost. It also gave the people Divine Guidance as to where it will be realized or made manifest, and that was in Samaria.

The prophets hear from God and speaks for God, they carry within their lions the **SHIFT ANOINTING**. The Prophets are anointed with the *'Mystery of the Shift.'* God will announce your Divine Shift through a Prophetic Voice. The prophets speak with divine wisdom. From their spiritual position they can pray and speak prophetically to release deliverance, healing and miracles to God's people it's from Kingly position and according to Proverbs 16:10, ***"The king speaks with divine wisdom, he must never judge unfairly."*** Get ready for the **"Shift,"** here the word of the Lord summoning you through these pages that something Greater is on the horizon for you, don't lose hope. Your current situation is not your destination. It is designed for you to push and birth out your Prophetic Destiny. It was designed to push you into your Promise. You just can't give up now or give into defeat or failure. Your dark place was designed to birth out of you **"The Greatness of the Shift"** and there are people awaiting your activation and manifestation into the shift, so they too can receive their Divine Release.

Chapter 3

Faith in Action

You cannot enter **"The Greatness of the Shift"** without walking by Faith. Hebrews 11:6 declares:

> ***"Without faith it is impossible to please him: for he that cometh to God must believe that he is, and that he is a rewarder of them that diligently seek him."***

Walking by faith cannot happen without prophetic revelation. Prophetic revelation is divine guidance from God. The prophets hear from God and speaks for God. Don't make the mistake as the King's Officer who doubted a Divine Promise coupled with Divine Instructions and Divine Guidance sent by God. Without Prophetic Revelation people become unrestrained and will fall under divine judgement. Elisha told the Kings Officer in 2 Kings 7: 2b ***"In fact, you shall see it with your eyes, but you shall not eat of it."*** When

Elisha declared their will be Divine Supplies by the Divine Hand of God the King's Officer doubted. Isaiah 55 says, God's word will not return to Him void of power. When Elisha prophesied God's deliverance, the King's Officer said it couldn't happen. The officer's faith and hope were gone. 2 Kings 7:14-16 shows evidence that the Prophetic Promise sent by God through Elijah to restore God's people manifested supernatural provision anyway even though the King's Officer did not believe the prophet. It really doesn't matter who doesn't believe in your promise or the prophetic word spoke to you, God is the Divine Orchestrator of **"The Shift"** and it is irrevocable and irreversible.

In the Book of chapter Exodus 12 their faith was now on trial for the **"Greatness of the Shift."** Your **"Faith in Action"** is always accompanied by Divine Direction or Instruction given by God. Hebrews Chapter 11 explicitly describe our forefathers the **"Pioneers of Faith"** obedience Divine Instructions and or a Divine Directions given to them. God withholds or withdraws His Glory when sin, disobedience or rebellion is evident. He releases His glory as a sign and a wonder to both believers and unbelievers so men would fear or revere Him as the one and only true God. But those who experience and operate in His tangible presence (His Glory) are those who trust Him and fear Him.

In Isaiah 6 when King Uzziah died, that was when Isaiah saw the Lord, high and lifted up. Isaiah's faith shifted him from a place of stagnation, and idolatry to a place of going beyond the veil into the Glory realm. He recognized that regardless of the accomplishments the Great King Uzziah had, the principles and standards of God still stands, and should not be broken. King Uzziah broke the Divine Order of the priesthood only given to the Levite tribe at the time and entered the most Holy Place to offer sacrifices unto the Lord a position only given to the priests of the Old Testament at the time.

You must walk by faith to shift from normalcy into the supernatural to activate the promises of God. When God gives you a certain portal to operate in or fulfill your assignment stay in your lane. Your pride can divinely reverse or deactivate your Divine Shift from the Lord. It's when we take our eyes off God and try to be like someone else that we become stuck in the process, because you are banking on their experiences only and what they have accomplished. Isaiah took his eyes off the Lord. **"Faith in Action"** requires the Uzziah's in our lives to be removed, eliminated or destroyed. If you have taken your eyes off the all-powerful, all knowing God it is time to refocus and reposition yourself. But what has become an Uzziah in your life must die.

The vital lesson learned from this scripture is that when King Uzziah died, the greater part of Isaiah's destiny began to emerge. **The Greatness of "THE SHIFT"** in your life will only emerge when you have made up your mind to move forward. You must be broken for God to move. You must be willing to lay down all the idols in your life. Regardless of the setbacks or opposing forces that surrounds you, arise and be awaken to the Prophetic Promise of God over your life. When your mind is transformed by the knowledge of who God is and you begin to search after the hidden treasures of God's word, according to Proverbs 2:5 then you will begin to **"understand the fear of the Lord and find the knowledge of God."**

You **"SHIFT"** cannot be made manifest without a Divine Release and a Divine Instructions. It was in the year that King Uzziah died that Isaiah saw the Lord high and lifted and the Glory of the Lord filled the temple. The Revealed Glory of the Lord births within you **The Mystery of the "SHIFT"** that will emerge from your life.

> *"In the year that king Uzziah died I saw also the Lord sitting upon a throne, high and lifted up, and his train filled the temple. ² Above it stood the seraphims: each one had six wings; with twain he covered his face, and with twain he covered his feet, and with twain he did fly. ³ And one cried unto another, and said, Holy, holy, holy, is the Lord of hosts: the whole earth is full of his glory. ⁴ And the posts of the door moved at the voice of him that cried, and the house was filled with smoke. ⁵ Then said I, Woe is me! For I am undone; because I am a man of unclean lips, and I dwell in the midst of a people of unclean lips: for mine eyes have seen the King, the Lord of hosts. ⁶ Then flew one of the seraphims unto me, having a live coal in his hand, which he had taken with the tongs from off the altar: ⁷ And he laid it upon my mouth, and said, Lo, this hath touched thy lips; and thine*

iniquity is taken away, and thy sin purged. ⁸ Also I heard the voice of the Lord, saying, Whom shall I send, and who will go for us? Then said I, Here am I; send me. ⁹ And he said, Go, and tell this people, Hear ye indeed, but understand not; and see ye indeed, but perceive not [Isaiah 6:1-9].

It's the box mentality way of living and thinking that became an hinderance to the predestinated plan of God for their lives with Pharaoh's yoke mentality to keep them stuck on stuck making bricks. *I prophecy to you that you are now shifting from making bricks to owning Brick Factory mentality in the name of Jesus.* God had to use by fire and by force Holy Ghost power and authority to catapult them into **"The Greatness of the Shift"** through the leading of Moses. Moses who was already cultivated, pruned and prepared to become a **"Carrier of the Shift."** He was chosen by God to deliver the Israelites out of bondage to their *"Tipping Point"* of moving forward into **"The Greatness of the Shift"** revealed in Exodus 12. The Divine instructions given to them in the beginning of the planned Exodus from Egypt was, after their deliverance they would come out and worship Him. In the interim, God's Divine Instructions to the Israelites after the tenth (10) plague was sent out against Pharaoh to force him to **"let God's people go."**

God appointed that on the night destined for their Divine Shift out of Egypt each family were instructed to kill a lamb. They were to eat it as directed and the blood from the lamb that was killed must be sprinkled on the doorpost to mark the houses of the Israelites as a symbol of protection. This was done to differentiate their houses from those of the Egyptians so that when the angel of the Lord sent to destroy the first-born of the Egyptians would pass over the houses marked by the blood of the lamb the Israelites would be saved. Exodus 12:23 declares through the oracle of God, Moses,

> **"For the Lord will pass through to strike the Egyptians; and when He sees the blood on the lintel and on the two doorposts, the Lord will pass over the door and not allow the destroyer to come into your houses to strike you."**

I prophesy to you that God is not silent forever, and in this hour and season of the Shift, the destroyer shall not strike you, nor your household, neither your possessions. God instructed them to put **"Faith in Action"** to experience deliverance and position them for **"The Greatness of the Shift."** Likewise, God will deliver you from your strong enemies. Your enemies trying to come after your blessings or promise is a stepping stone for you to enter the **Greatness of the Shift.** No one can kill or destroy what God has purposed and destined to live. Surely goodness and mercy shall follow you all the days of your life when you trust God's plan for your life regardless of the pitfalls, difficult test or trials.

As we discovered in Exodus 12, the same people in Egypt that oppressed them had to release to them articles of silver, articles of gold and clothing. Exodus 12:36 declares**, "And the Lord had given the people favor in the sight of the Egyptians."** *I prophecy to you that the ones that made your lives a living hell will not only watch you exit but also release will command the blessings of the Lord upon your life from a place that seemed like defeat into* **"The Greatness of the Shift."**

Whatever your struggles are, like the four (4) lepers at the gate you are a candidate for **"The Greatness of the Shift"** and no power on earth can block what God has Supernaturally released under an **"Open Heaven"** for your life.

Sometimes we become preoccupied with problems when we should be looking for opportunities. Instead of focusing on the negatives, we should develop an attitude of expectancy. To say that God cannot rescue someone or to imply that a situation is impossible demonstrates a lack of faith. **"SHIFT"** your thinking today and **"Refuse to Die Here."** The King's Officer refuse to believe that a **"Shift"** was soon coming, but the windows of Heaven were opened the very next day.

> ***"So, a seah of fine flour was sold for a shekel, and two seahs of barley for a shekel, according to the word of the Lord. 17 Now the king had appointed the officer on whose hand he leaned to have charge of the gate. But the people trampled him in the gate, and he died, just as the man of God had said, who spoke when the king came down to him. 18 So it happened just as the man of God had spoken to the king, saying, "Two seahs of barley for a shekel, and a seah of fine flour for a***

shekel, shall be sold tomorrow about this time in the gate of Samaria."
19 Then that officer had answered the man of God, and said, "Now look, if the Lord would make windows in heaven, could such a thing be?" And he had said, "In fact, you shall see it with your eyes, but you shall not eat of it." 20 And so it happened to him, for the people trampled him in the gate, and he died" [2 Kings 7:16-20].

I prophecy to you that the Lord shall swallow whatever is trying to swallow you, you have the spirit that Conquers and Win, through Jesus Christ. Get ready for Enlargement of Territories. This is your comeback season from Leper into Greater. This is your comeback season for your land of increase. This is your comeback season for your land of Mega Blessings. This is the season that the wicked hand against you will rot and the Divine Hand of God shall propel *you into **"The Greatness of the Shift."** Those who did not believe the promise over your life or the prophetic word spoken through you, shall see the manifestation of **"The Greatness of the SHIFT"** in your life and it shall confound then. I decree and declare that they shall see it but not partake of it.*

Help me prophesy: -

"At this time tomorrow" a Divine Door of Opportunity shall be opened to me for financial release in every area of my life. This time tomorrow showers of blessings shall perpetually flow in every area of my life. This time tomorrow the Divine Hand of God is reversing every failure into success. This time tomorrow I shall encounter my Divine Connection to my promise and breakthrough. This time tomorrow it shall be made manifest as the mouth of the Lord has spoken, in Jesus name."

This time tomorrow is indicating that **"After This"** day and season of turbulence and tribulation, there shall be a continuous flow of miracles in your life. I prophesy to you today, ***"Your struggles are a set up for a miracle." You are next in-line for a MIRACLE, THIS TIME TOMORROW."*** Receive it NOW in Jesus name.

Chapter 4

DREAM AGAIN TO SHIFT

Whatever God has anointed you and preserved you to endure as a test or walk through as a very dark season of your life would have caused others to drown. When you find yourself at a crossroad situation where it seems there is insurmountable setbacks as if you are going backwards. The only way forward is to breakthrough that dark place or Red Sea and the only thing you must stand on is the Prophetic Promise from the Lord.

You must be very careful to walk in obedience to the Prophetic Promise over your life to prevent the spirit of abortion or miscarriage to your destiny. If you feel like you are at a crossroad where your dream is getting ready to die or you have suffered loss in the form of a dream you had, whether it be marriage, a miscarriage, business idea or spiritual goal, I want to encourage you to **"Dream Again."** You have to **"Dream Again to Shift."**

Romans 8:28 says, **"And we know that God causes everything to work together[a] for the good of those who love God and are called according to his purpose for them."**

When God gives you, a clear word stands on it. When God makes a covenant with you, He will not turn back on His promises.

"The Lord replied, "Listen, I am making a covenant with you in the presence of all your people. I will perform miracles that have never been performed anywhere in all the earth or in any nation. And all the people around you will see the power of the Lord—the awesome power I will display for you" [Exodus 34:10].

God promise to you that not only will you experience the Greatness of the Shift but all the people around you will see the power of the Lord manifesting greatness in your life.

"Dream Again to Shift" means you must practice to P.U.S.H. yourself. It means putting away your feeling, denying yourself [flesh]. If you wait until you feel like doing, you will likely never accomplish your dream. You must have a **NOW FAITH** mentality to see the fullness of the **"Prophetic Promise"** activated in your life. If you wait until you feel like praising God, you will never likely get a breakthrough. All God requires for the fulfillment of the promise is your participation, meaning your obedience is required. Zacharias and Elizabeth were barren for many years and were now very old when God manifested their Shift. They did not turn to other gods or idols but rather they maintained continuity of faith by serving faithfully as priest in the temple **"Praying Again Until"** the Greatness of the Shift manifest in their lives.

"Pay close attention to all my instructions. You must not call on the name of any other gods. Do not even speak their names" [Exodus 23:13].

I implore you through this book, do not turn to other sources or idols, wait on God's Divine Guidance or instructions for He has already released ***"The Angel and the Promise."***

"Behold I send an angel before you into the place which I have prepared. Beware of him and obey his voice, do not provoke Him, for he will not pardon your transgressions: - For my name is in Him" [Exodus 23:20].

God has already assigned angels to help you and to carry you into the promise. God is preparing you for greater. I pray for a stirring in your spirit and within your lions as you read on to **"Dream Again to Shift,"** because though the vision tarry wait for it, for when it manifest, it shall surely speak and not lie.

> ***"For the vision is yet for an appointed time, but at the end it shall speak, and not lie: though it tarry, wait for it; because it will surely come, it will not tarry"*** [Habakkuk 2].

When it manifests you will experience **"The Greatness of the Shift"** and those around you will know the hand of the Lord is upon your life. Sometime what God desires to release to us seems slow or delayed but we must trust and patiently wait for the manifestation of it. Psalm 31:1 says, **"In you oh Lord, I take refuge."** This means to trust God, depend on his protection and dwell in Him for He is a safety net. When the disciples were told of the resurrection of Christ it seemed idle to them, so they did not believe. Luke 24:11 says, **"But these words seemed to them an idle tale, and they did not believe."** You must believe and continually prayer and not faint to see the promises of the Lord manifest in your life.

Where God's Glory dwells birthing is inevitable. Zacharias was a man who lived in the Glory of the Lord. He spent quality time serving as a priest in the temple faithfully and his wife Elizabeth was very old and was also barren. Luke 1:5-7 reveals that:

> **"There was in the days of Herod, the king of Judaea, a certain priest named Zacharias, of the course of Abia: and his wife was of the daughters of Aaron, and her name was Elisabeth. ⁶And they were both righteous before God, walking in all the commandments and ordinances of the LORD blameless. ⁷And they had no child, because that**

Elisabeth was barren, and they both were now well stricken in years."

Just because you are righteous, it doesn't mean you won't have challenges, oppositions or setbacks. But because of their faithfulness and obedience before God, there was a Prophetic Override and release into their lives I can only describe as the **"Greatness of the Shift."** No matter how long and hard it may appear or seem your destination into destiny don't give up. You must persevere because greatness takes time to be developed. It is during the darkest period, like the midnight hour is when the breaking of dawn appears. I declare to you your daybreak is on the horizon.

Zacharias and Elizabeth kept serving faithfully and loving the Lord continually in spite the odds that were against them having children. The **"Suddenlies of God"** manifested while their eyes were stayed on the Lord and serving wholeheartedly as described in Luke 1:8-11

"One day Zechariah was serving God in the Temple, for his order was on duty that week. 9 As was the custom of the priests, he was

chosen by lot to enter the sanctuary of the Lord and burn incense. 10 While the incense was being burned, a great crowd stood outside, praying."

"While Zechariah was in the sanctuary, an angel of the Lord appeared to him, standing to the right of the incense altar. 12 Zechariah was shaken and overwhelmed with fear when he saw him. 13 But the angel said, "Don't be afraid, Zechariah! God has heard your prayer. Your wife, Elizabeth, will give you a son, and you are to name him John. 14 You will have great joy and gladness, and many will rejoice at his birth."

The Greatness of the Shift in your life can take place Suddenly. I feel a Shift right now in the Glory Realm, hallelujah, receive your miracle in the name of Jesus. You Shift can take place suddenly just like God did for Zechariah and Elizabeth in Luke chapter 1. You Shift can come suddenly just as he did for me.

Later in this book I will share my miraculous story of the birth of my children when the odds were against me. So regardless of what the biological clock says, when you live in the glory, miracles become your second nature. Meaning that, miracles will always be a continuous flow or occurrence in your life.

Where God's Glory dwells birthing is just the second nature. Zacharias was getting ready to experience **"The Greatness of the Shift"** suddenly. Your **"Suddenlies of God"** encounter, comes after a great period of afflictions, trials, test or setback. Where God glory *dwells "The Birthing of your Prophetic Destiny"* shall manifest.

I read an article recently that explains that every baby born is considered a miracle. But a true miracle is one that beats the odds against it and still manifest. 10-25% of clinically recognized pregnancies end in miscarriage. Miscarriage is a term used for a pregnancy that ends on its own, within the first 20 weeks of gestation. Chromosomal abnormalities are the cause of a damaged egg or sperm cell or are due to a problem at the time that the zygote went through the division process. Other causes of miscarriage include (but are not limited to): -

- Hormonal problems, infections or maternal health problems
- Lifestyle (i.e. smoking, drug use, malnutrition, excessive caffeine and exposure to radiation or toxic substances)
- Implantation of the egg into the uterine lining does not occur properly
- Maternal age
- Maternal trauma.

DNA of Destiny

The DNA of Destiny starts with a seed. A plant grows from a seed sown into the ground or earth. It is then watered and managed by a caregiver or farmer to ensure weeds or bugs does not infest the crop or plant. When tending to the seeds, he constantly nurtures it with water and the right nutrient for healthy growth.

What is the essence of sharing about abortion or miscarriage this soon in the book, is to alert you that when God is birthing something within be very careful how you handle the revelation or your Prophetic Word which is a seed. You must nurture the seed, our Prophetic Promise constantly with the Word. Jesus is the Word, meaning bread of life, living water. The woman at the well transformation into **"The Greatness of the Shift"** could not manifest until she accepted the living water from Jesus with a promise of activation of greatness in her life. In just some very simple yet profound words Jesus announces to her **"The Greatness of the Shift."**

> *"Jesus replied, "If you only knew the gift God has for you and who you are speaking to, you would ask me, and I would give you living water."13 Jesus replied, "Anyone who drinks this water will soon become thirsty again. 14 But those who drink the water I give will never be thirsty again. It becomes a fresh, bubbling spring within them, giving them eternal life."15 "Please, sir," the woman said, "give me this water! Then I'll never be thirsty again, and I won't have to come here to get water"* [St. John 4:12-15].

She was willing to surrender to his will and give up her old life style when He unfold to her,

her history. Like I said earlier, God will use your History for his glory.

Royal Access is the DNA of Destiny into your inheritance, but you must exercise unshakable faith. The Holy Spirit was given to us as a Divine Enabler to help spiritual cultivate and produce the DNA of Destiny for our lives. Your Roya Access is activated and grow or expand by how you handle the word given to you as a Prophetic Promise. How you handle the word given to you as a Prophetic Promise will determine if the spiritual baby lives or dies. This book entitled, "The Greatness of the Shift" comes in a Series, and Part 2 will be more in depth as I believe the Greatness of the Shift is a Global Mandate releasing a Clarion Call and summons to those who are chosen by God to be Carriers of the Shift not to lose hope or give up on their dream and destiny. I believe after this November 2018 Prophetic Shift Conference as this book is launched that, this Shift Conference shall manifest into Mega Global Shift, not only in the United States of America but we shall carry this Shift Anointing Oil from Nations to Nations.

Your Destiny is divinely transferred to your spirit out of the womb of the Supernatural by the Holy Spirit from the God's Throne Room. As you will see later as I began to share and expound on the story of Zechariah's announcement of the Birthing of Destiny for Him and Elizabeth you will see that he was at the right place and at the right time in the presence of the Lord. It initially, becomes a seed through you Divine Impartation and receiving the word of God [**The Prophetic Promise**]. You must believe it, receive it and act upon it. This seed is tried by fire until you grow into maturity to handle the greatness the Lord is calling you into and walk in it. That's when the manifestation and ultimate birthing of your purpose, destiny, breakthrough, and miracles take place.

> *"But we have this treasure in earthen vessels, that the excellence of the power may be of God and not of us. ⁸ We are hard-pressed on every side, yet not crushed; we are perplexed, but not in despair; ⁹ persecuted, but not forsaken; struck down, but not destroyed— ¹⁰ always carrying about in the body the dying of the Lord Jesus, that the life of Jesus also may be manifested in our body"* [2 Corinthians 4:7-10].

You must go through the process where the seed dies first as in the plant life cycle before it will begin to sprout or show any evidence of life pressing through the earth into the light with leaves and branches. You may experience several stages of changes or shifts before the greatness of your Divine Destiny is completely activated.

Prophetic Reset to Restore

If you are at the point where you feel like you want to throw in the towel, feeling discouraged or disheartened fear not. A promise is a promise from God, and it cannot be revoked by man nor any other force. Whatever came in the way to intercept your promise God wants to reset to restore you for the Greatness of the Shift. Sometimes you feel like you want to let go, but the **"Greatness of the Shift"** requires perseverance. You must be willing to P.U.S.H. Persevere Until the Shift Happens. God desires to reset your life to restore it. Greatness takes time, and perseverance is a vital key to unlocking greatness. Even our Savior our main source and example of perseverance had to endure the painful crucifixion for our Royal Access into our Inheritance.

- **Greatness means**: Radical obedience even during the fiery trials and challenges, God requires your perseverance and consistency into the next dimension.
- **Perseverance means**: Determination, persistency or diligence.
- The question is how bad you want it. How bad do you want the Prophetic Unlocking of **"The Greatness of the Shift"** in your life?
- How determined are you to walk into your Destiny?
- How determined are you to see the fulfillment of the Prophetic Promise from God activated in your life?

You begin to gain or build momentum called progression when you keep pushing or moving forward. Progression is a feeling of endurance and perseverance to a place where you cannot hold back or be still or else the baby will die. You can read more about **"Perseverance to Progression"** in my first book, entitled, *"Awake to Your Destiny"* available on Amazon.com or through our ministry.

God desires to reset your life to be restored so that you can enter all that He has for you. But if you give up, you will not experience the Greatness of the Shift. There is a Prophetic Reset of God's promises in your life. Forget the former things for behold God is doing a new thing. Shut out the voices of Peninnah, the naysayers like Sanballat's and the Tobias's, shut out the ones who *"nay,"* and connect with the power of the Holy Ghost that announces, **"YEA, though I walk through the valley of the shadow of death, I will fear no evil..."** Say YEA, somebody, Hallelujah Glory!!!

Watch in this hour what you speak and watch who you open to. God is about to turn it. Somebody better shout *"He Turned It."* He is about to Prophetically Reset to Restore you into the Greatness of the Shift. God is about to turn your womb to naturally or spiritually give birth. Sometimes demonic attack comes up against the Prophetic Promise divinely ordained by God for your life. Therefore, just like the Lord did for Joseph, he will do for you. God shall **"Reset to Restore"** every promise he has made to you. Sometime those you share your story or promise with will begin to doubt especially when many years have passed. That is because they have become familiar with your circumstances. If you abide in Christ and stay focus on the promise, it shall be done. Remain confident that He will fulfill every promise to you. Consistent faith. God reminded him of the seed of promise he would give him. Even though Sarah lost hope on the promise Abraham faith caused God to **"Reset to Restore the Prophetic Promise."**

God is still healing, He is still delivering and He's about to turn things around in your favor. The Courts of Heaven has come into our atmosphere to turn things in our favor. The next court hearing for someone reading, it will be in your favor. **"Prophetic Reset to Restore"** is an indication that Jehovah has the final say in your life. So here is a Prophetic Decree and Declaration below you can pray as a release. This will help you break free and mentality prepare you to receive and captivate all that is written in this book as a Divine Instruction and Rhema Word from the Lord to reassure you, help you and guide you into the ***"Greatness of the Shift."***

Prophetic Reset to Restore Prayer Declaration

Forgive me Lord if every decision that I've made when I was tired and spiritual weak and had no prayer life with you that has cause discombobulation or blockages in my life! I pray that you will Reset to Restore my Life accordingly your Divine Purpose and will Pre-Destined before the foundation of the earth was ever formed in the matchless name of Jesus! In my life, be Glorified thank you for Wisdom which is the principal thing to accomplish this New Season and Fresh Start in you Lord! Let the Consuming Fire of the Holy Spirit confiscate every demonic altar and satellites right now and I declare every area of my life is free from the yoked formed out of rational thinking and actions even contributed by negative associations & influences. Shut every door that have been opened in ignorance to the enemy and I declare and declare that I go free, my family go free, my finances go free! I decree and declare every promise God has given to me is Prophetically Reset to Restore. I decree and declare that my setback is working a greater comeback. I decree and declare this is my moment for Prophetic Reset to Restore and I will struggle no more, I will soar. I decree and declare I will not only be a survivor, but I shall become a Kingdom Shift, a Carrier of the Shift. I decree and declare that my problem is an invitation to change and I anticipate it, I believe it and I expect it. I decree and declare that my Shift is in my

Seed, for my seed carries within my Supernatural Harvest and my Destiny. Therefore, I will not hold back my time, gifts, services, money or resources from advancing the Kingdom of God. I decree and declare that my problems are an invitation for the Greatness of the Shift. I decree and declare Prophetic RESET to RESTORE is in full effect in every area of my life in the Jesus matchless name. Amen.

Chapter 5

The Prophetic Announcement of Greatness

I am here to prophetically announce to you that your purpose shall not be aborted. Repeat after me, **"I Will Not Abort My Purpose Destiny is Calling Me."** I am **"Destined for Greatness"** and God will not stop my purpose midstream. My purpose shall not be aborted, and I shall experience the full manifestation of the Greatness of the Shift.

But I also hear God saying: Watch and pray

> Luke 18:1 says **"1 declares, 1 And he spake a parable unto them to this end, that men ought always to pray, and not to faint;"**

- **Prayer**: is to implore, plead, beg, ask, entreat, request, urge [push for], call upon, advocate [supporter, backer, promoter, promoter].

- **Faint**: To pass out, to become or grow feeble, lose strength or color. Faint is to sink into dejection, to lose courage or spirit. Faint is to become depressed or despondent.

When the Lord releases a **"Prophetic Announcement"** of His Divine Plan over your life don't abort it. **Abort means**: - stop midstream, to call a halt, terminate, to abandon, or call off. He sends a Prophetic Announcement [Message or Declaration] to reassurance you and to release you from the feeling of growing feeble, losing strength and becoming dejected.

> *"Be strong and courageous, for you are the one who will lead these people to possess all the land I swore to their ancestors I would give them. 7 Be strong and very courageous. Be careful to obey all the instructions Moses gave you. Do not deviate from them, turning either to the right or to the left. Then you will be successful in everything you do"* [Joshua 1:6-7].

When these words of encouragement came to Joshua from the Lord it was simply telling him that, even though these plans are forthcoming, while you wait to implement or see the fulfillment of these Divine Instructions and Directions do not stop midstream, do not get frustrated **"Persevere Until the Shift Happens."** Joshua immediately summons the people into a prayer and fasting to consecrate themselves for the **"Greatness of the Shift."** When God is about to do something great, it is generally followed by a **"Prophetic Announcement."** Announcement means, statement, declaration, proclamation or message. Prophetic Announcement was evident in the beginning when God creative explosion manifested on the earth in Genesis chapter 1:1-3. God spoke what He wanted to exist, and it was activated from His mouth.

> *"In the beginning God created the heavens and the earth. 2 The earth was formless and empty, and darkness covered the deep waters. And the Spirit of God was hovering over the surface of the waters.*
> *3 Then God said, "Let there be light," and there was light. 4 And*

> ***God saw that the light was good. Then he separated the light from the darkness. 5 God called the light "day" and the darkness "night." And evening passed, and morning came, marking the first day."***

The first three (3) verse of Genesis chapter one (1) set the tone of the **"Greatness of the Shift"** that was manifested in the earth that allowed all creation to exist. The earth was filled with darkness, was without shape and empty. But I want you to recognize from the creation of this world that **"Greatness"** is birthed out of darkness. Once **"The Greatness of the Shift"** is activated nothing can turn it back. The moment the Holy Spirit open its mouth and made the **"Prophetic Announcement"** [Declaration], ***"Let there be light"***, without a shadow of a doubt there was light. Once the lights were turn on literally by His mighty acts and power it was irrevocable. It could not be turned off, it was final.

The next five to six (5-6) days the Lord was busy generating the Divine Plan of creation. When He did that, He instituted man on the sixth day, to be a replica of Himself. He imparted to Adam and Eve the Royal Access and it was their Inheritance, which was and still is the DNA of Destiny for **"The Greatness of the SHIFT."** Royal Access to your Inheritance was already predestined from Genesis 1. But the fall of man brought about a Greater Shift in the form of Christ to restore us back to our rightful place and promise in the Lord [Genesis 1:26-28, Ephesians 2:4-9]

> *"And God said, Let us make man in our image, after our likeness: and let them have dominion over the fish of the sea, and over the fowl of the air, and over the cattle, and over all the earth, and over every creeping thing that creepeth upon the earth. 27 So God created man in his own image, in the image of God created he him; male and female created he them. 28 And God blessed them, and God said unto them, Be fruitful, and multiply, and replenish the earth, and subdue it: and have dominion over the fish of the sea, and over the fowl of the air, and over every living thing that moveth upon the earth"* [Genesis 1:26-28].

> *"But God, who is rich in mercy, for his great love wherewith he loved us, 5 even when we were dead in sins,*

hath quickened us together with Christ, (by grace ye are saved;) 6 and hath raised us up together, and made us sit together in heavenly places in Christ Jesus: 7 that in the ages to come he might shew the exceeding riches of his grace in his kindness toward us through Christ Jesus. 8 For by grace are ye saved through faith; and that not of yourselves: it is the gift of God: 9 not of works, lest any man should boast. 10 For we are his workmanship, created in Christ Jesus unto good works, which God hath before ordained that we should walk in them" [Ephesians 2:4-9].

"The Greatness of the Shift" was ordained by God that you should walk in it. God created us to be reflection of His greatness. We are made in His own image and likeness which reflects His glory. Which means we have in us God's DNA to fulfill a Divine Purpose predestined by Him. As we walk out these purposes in obedience it will lead us into the Unlocking of Greatness.

Don't Be Afraid God is on Your Boat

God predestined us with the ability to reflect His character in how to patiently love and remain faithful during our season of waiting and enduring hard trials. Remind yourself when you are feeling faint hearted. Don't lose hope. God comes to restore some things that you gave up on. Remember that, *"Having God in the boat doesn't mean that you'll not face any storm. But it means that no storm can sink your boat! Walk in faith and you'll never walk alone"* [Author: Unknown].

When you take a step-in faith following the Divine Direction God wants to take you, it doesn't necessarily mean there won't be roadblocks or storms. It doesn't necessarily mean that it will be smooth sailing when God releases a Prophetic Announcement for the **"Greatness of the Shift"** in your life. If you feel like you are in one of those dark storms, Jesus is on your boat taking you into the **"Greatness of the Shift."** There will be challenges in the way to try to bombard you from the enemy, but you must remain confident that you are following God's path. Rest assured that God watches over His word to perform it. The Greatness of the Shift is marked by suffering, persecution and trials.

> *"We can rejoice, too, when we run into problems and trials, for we know that they are good for us— they help us learn to be patient. ⁴ And patience develops strength of character in us and helps us trust God more each time we use it until finally our hope and faith are strong and steady"* [Romans 5:3-4].

Before God releases you into greatness you will go through a series of test to prove if your faith is genuine, but not to worry, as you remain confident and trust Him, He is on your boat.

What Zacharias and Elizabeth was about to give birth to could not be polluted not even by a hint of negativity even from their own spirit. At times when God speaks a word to us and we don't see it manifest immediately we tend to panic. After waiting a long period of time, our instinct is to become overwhelmed by our struggles and then we begin to wrestle. But I encourage you, don't wrestle with the newness you are sensing, and the revelation God sends to you unexpectedly to announce your new season called **"The Greatness of the Shift."**

Luke Chapter 1 reveals in-depth to Zacharias that, the child they were about to conceive shall be a forerunner to prepare the way of the Lord. God will not ignore the history of your past or your test. He will use it to propel you into greatness. May, I remind you again the greater your warfare, it is the greater manifestation of God's power and glory in your life. It wasn't just an ordinary child the Lord was supernaturally impregnating their loins to produce, it was a **"Kingdom Shifter."** One who would go forth with boldness and authority to prepare, save, deliver and transform nations by the power of the Holy Spirit.

Luke 1:15 affirms what I just shared saying,

> ***"For he will be great in the eyes of the Lord. He must never touch wine or other alcoholic drinks. He will be filled with the Holy Spirit, even before his birth. 16 And he will turn many Israelites to the Lord their God. 17 He will be a man with the spirit and power of Elijah."***

Do not count out your test because of frustration or suffering. I share with you what the Lord reveal to me, just this morning,

October 24, 2018 by a simple scripture verse we frequently pray and memorized as believers.

> ***"Be anxious for nothing, but in everything by prayer and supplication, with thanksgiving, let your requests be made known to God; 7 and the peace of God, which surpasses all understanding, will guard your hearts and minds through Christ"*** [Philippians 4:6-7].

I ask the Lord, what is the significance of this in my situation right now. He said, I will keep your heart and mind as you wait. I said wow! A lot of our mental fatigue and frustration is not so much when and how it will manifest. But rather, it is our refusal to surrender to the Lords will. We need to yield of our body, mind, soul and spirit to the Holy Spirit so that He can completely immerse us into His glory. When we are not totally yielded or submitted to the Lords that is what cause most of our mental fatigue and frustration. When you are completely immersed into His glory, that's when the Greatness of the Shift begins to take form or shape in our lives.

The Prophetic Announcement of the promise begins to take shape as it is released to perform that which it was sent to do. When you are completely aligned and ready for the Prophetic Announcement of the Shift it becomes unstoppable, it is irreversible, it is non-transferable because your DNA of Destiny is written all over it. No one else in the temple that day could get what was Divinely release to Zacharias and Elizabeth. This will be revealed in-depth later in the book.

It was their set time of favor and no matter what the enemy tried to do, it was their divine moment for **"The Greatness of the Shift."** I am here to prophetically announce to you that no one else can receive or wear your Mantle no matter how hard they pray for it out of jealousy. Man cannot undo what was predestined and birthed in the spirit realm for you. Hence, why we pattern to pray, thy Kingdom come, they will be done on earth as it is in heaven. We blame the devil too much and give him too much credit when we are struggling. When in fact God just want us to stay calm and never waiver.

Hold on to the profession of your faith without wavering for he is faithful who promised. You sow for your harvest continually when you see it or don't see it. God is restoring the promise over your life and He will never lose interest in the promise He has declared over your life. Those who don't expect anything great to come forth from your life shall be ashamed by the Prophetic Announcement and manifestation of Gods promise over your life. What is about to manifest in your life it's a God thing and it's a Supernatural Destiny Shift that cannot be altered. It Is your perseverance until the shift happens [P.U.S.H.] that will bring forth the fullness of your Destiny.

Whatever confronts you right now in your life as a threat, challenge or attack is an indicator of the size of your breakthrough and the anointing you will carry. As you patiently wait for your change [The Shift], all God requires is your obedience to His divine will and the divine instructions He is giving you in this season. In Luke chapter I it was quite evident that Zechariah and Elizabeth were making every effort to P.U.S.H. Persevere Until the Shift Happens. Here Zechariah and Elizabeth waited patiently, and it wasn't certain in the natural they were past the age of child bearing according to Luke 1:7, **"They had no children because Elizabeth was unable to conceive, and they were both very old."** Elizabeth was barren. Not to mention, Luke adds the detail that they were both very old, meaning that they could not expect any change in their situation.

For Elizabeth, being childless in your old age would be painful and lonely; but during this time, she remained faithful to God. Don't give upon God, remain faithful, as you continually pursuit after His perfect will and plan for your life. In fact, I want to tell some folk also don't give up on what God is not through with yet. We tend to write people off quickly when their situation seemed terminal or barren. By doing that we reveal that we know about him but really don't know who He is when we place limitation on what, where and when God can move. I say the same thing to you about your situation **P.U.S.H. [Persevere Until the Shift Happens]** by:

- Keep hope alive while you wait by worshipping while you wait.
- Keep praying while you wait.
- Keep serving faithfully while you wait.
- Keep walking in obedience to every Divine Instruction given to you by God while you wait because suddenly your Shift will manifest.
- While you are waiting on your keep on sowing until it shifts
- While you are waiting on keep on praying like Zacharias until it shifts.

- While you're waiting keep on worshipping like Job until it shifts.
- While you are waiting keep on worshipping and praying like Hannah.

Chapter 6

The Suddenlies of God

Just like, Hannah, Zechariah and Elizabeth, **P.U.S.H.** [Persevere Until the Shifts Happens]. "**Don't Abort your Purpose Destiny is Calling You into the Greatness of the Shift**." Your shift into greatness can happen suddenly. In Chapter 8 I will share my personal testimony of conceiving and giving birth to triplet and two (2) years later another child miraculously and suddenly. When I exegete the text, it is evident that the Greatness of the Shift is the Suddenlies of God. It happens unexpectedly and uncalculated by any human efforts or reasoning, it is Supernatural. Many are trying to get their release, but it is a struggle because it defies natural reasoning, or rational and the human spirit cannot fathom something supernatural. Don't limit God, only yield to God. The Book of Luke 1:8 not only reveals and confirms the Suddenlies of God. This chapter also demonstrate graphically that the activation of the Greatness of the Shift happens suddenly.

"One day Zechariah was serving God in the Temple, for his order was on duty that week. 9 As was the custom of the priests, he was chosen by lot to enter the sanctuary of the Lord and burn incense."

Two key things to point out is:

- The location was significant. The question is, are you in the right place and position.
- And secondly there is a set time. Your right place and position prepare you for your set time.

Habakkuk 2 also reveals that Habakkuk was on the watch tower when God came to encourage him that, *"though the vision tarry wait for it."* Many move out of position because they were not chosen for a part or assignment. Bur Zacharias showed up to the temple whether the lot was cast for him to serve our not. When God announces a Divine Conference like this one, we have annually called **"The Shift"** Conference please show up. The custom in those days is that incense was burned in the temple. Herod expanded and beautified the Jerusalem Temple, but his sole intension was not for spiritual reasons but more so for political reasons. When he helped the Jews, it was to please his superiors who appointed him King of the Jews. Herod was only half Jewish, so what he did was for political purposes not because he cared for the Jews. But God always intervene no matter who is set over a region or territory to make decisions as seen in Zacharias's story, nothing can hold back the hand of God when it is your time for **"The Greatness of the Shift."**

The Jewish priest was a minister of God who worked at the temple to manage its upkeep naturally, as well as spiritually they taught the people the word of God and direct the worship services. It was during this time when Zacharias and Elizabeth Shift took place there were about 20,0000 priests throughout the country. That's a lot of ministers at any one time. But, when it's your season and your time, like the woman with the issue of blood she pressed through the crowd and touched the hem of Jesus' garment. When it is your season and your time, it is irrevocable, no matter how many, 20,000 or more surrounds you.

The 20,000 Jewish Priest were divided into 24 separate groups of about 1000 each according to David's instructions (1 Chronicles

24:3-19). Zacharias was a member of the group called Abijah, were on duty this week. Each morning a priest was to enter the Holy Place in the temple and burn incense. The priest would cast lots to decide who would enter the inner sanctuary, and one day the lot fell to Zacharias. But it was not by chance that He was chosen that day to enter the Holy Place. Let me encourage you to hold on to the profession of your faith because unshakable faith wins and will always win. It is God almighty himself that guides history to prepare the way for Jesus. The manifestation of Zacharias and Elizabeth divine release to bear a son called John was to prepare the announcement and to become the forerunner of the coming forth of the Savior of the World Jesus Christ, Son of the living God.

    You are chosen to be a part of this great move of God in this end time. God will use your history of enduring hardship as a good shoulder, through afflictions, painful trials and struggles to catapult you into the Greatness of the Shift. You will have a testimony and the manifestation of glory to transform lives in your family, school, business arena where you conduct business, in your local church, community. For a remnant **"The Greatness of the Shift"** in your life shall release you on international platforms to declare, announce and proclaim supernatural shifts in the lives of people globally who are groaning and waiting for the manifestation of the sons of God. Get ready for your **"Greatness of the Shift."**

Take a lesson from Zacharias and Elizabeth life as you are getting ready for the Shift in your life. They didn't just merely go through church rituals or motions following Gods precepts, they backed it up by outward actions and compliance with inward obedience. Their obedience was from the heart and that is why they are called "righteous before God. Can God call you righteous before Him. Isaiah 1:19 says, *"If ye be willing and obedient, ye shall eat the good of the land."* I'm sure they were desperate for a change in their lives and based on Zacharias reaction it was surprising and shocking to the point where the angel had to release a command to make him dumb to not mess up **"The Greatness of the Shift"** that was about to take place in their lives. For some, like Zacharias you talk too much. therefore, the Lord will not reveal or unfold certain particulars to your destiny until the fullness of time because you talk too much.

Mega Blessings

God answers prayers in his own set time and prophetic calendar for our lives. He works in impossible situations as in Elizabeth's age and barrenness to bring about the fulfillment of a Prophetic Promise concerning the Messiah, Jesus Christ. God can suddenly turn your trials and test into **"Mega Blessings"** suddenly. God will turn your impossibilities into supernatural possibilities just like He did for me when the medical report said, two (2) miscarriages, and it seemed like my hope was gone because my doctor spoke doomed over me, as revealed later in this book. But God uses that situation to turn my life around into "The **"Greatness of the Shift"** for **"Mega-Blessings."**

My shift was Mega with the birth of the triplet Abigail, Aaron and Nathaniel and two (2) years later another child my last-born Joshua, to announce to earth, God does things in Mega style. Mega means extraordinary, unprecedented, and it is supernatural. If you are reading this book, it's because the Lord is preparing you for greatness.

I prophecy to you that you are Destined for Greatness. I decree and declare that your shift shall be Greater than you can even ask or imagine. I decree and declare that your Shift shall be a Mega Shift. I prophecy that your shift shall be a Supernatural Shift. I decree and declare to you, I once in a life time opportunity shall come to you just as the Lord did for Zacharias and Elizabeth.

This was a once-in-a-lifetime opportunity for Zacharias to be in the temple. Lots were cast in Luke 1:9, to determine who would have the privilege of burning incense in the most Holy Place during the hour of prayer (Exodus 30:7-8). According to the Jewish Mishnah, this was a rare privilege.

I announce to you what God is doing through these annual conferences we host, November, March-April and June months are a set up for a remnant to experience a supernatural shift into their Divine release, miracles and breakthroughs. I believe those who wrote you off as no good and nothing good can come from your life will be put to shame. God is getting ready to open a door for you called *'Divine Opportunity Door,'* that will prophetically unlock blessings, and divine connections to take you into your Dream, Purpose and Destiny. The Lord will use your impossible situation to accelerate you into: **"The Greatness of the Shift."** What once brought scorned and rejection from those familiar with your situation the Lord will turn it around into unprecedent favor and overflowing miracles and blessings. The Lord will use your season of what seem like defeats to bring about the fulfillment of your Prophetic Destiny and Prophetic Promises from the Lord.

I encourage you to be open to the Lord for there is a **"Shift"** taking place right now in your atmosphere. You must be open to what God can do in impossible situations and you must wait for God to work in His way and in His time. So that, when God finally show up be careful like I said not to doubt just be open in His presence. Luke 1:11-13 reveals what happen to Zacharias when the angel announced the message of the Prophetic Promise of giving birth to them.

> *"While Zacharias was in the sanctuary, an angel of the Lord appeared to him, standing to the right of the incense altar. 12 Zechariah was shaken and overwhelmed with fear when he saw him. 13 But the angel said, "Don't be afraid, Zechariah! God has heard your prayer. Your wife, Elizabeth, will give*

you a son, and you are to name him John."

The angel referred to Zacharias' petition (Luke 1:13), probably for a child. Zacharias' response was the same as Abraham's in Luke 1:18 compare to Genesis 15:8. He said, **"how shall I know this? For I am an old man, and my wife is well advanced in years."** But with God anything is possible. Zacharias clearly doubted because they were both very old and his wife was obviously barren. But the angel answered and said,

> **"Then the angel said, "I am Gabriel! I stand in the very presence of God. It was he who sent me to bring you this good news! 20 But now, since you didn't believe what I said, you will be silent and unable to speak until the child is born. For my words will certainly be fulfilled at the proper time"** [Luke 1:19-20].

Don't allow your doubts to overshadow your **"Shift."** Don't allow others opinion or doubts overshadow your Shift. Because Zacharias doubted the angel's word God caused him to go mute (dumb) **"Until the day these things take place, because you did not**

believe my words which will be fulfilled in their own time." For what God promises, He deliver. And God will deliver on time. When God sends his divine messenger to release your change as be implore you to be open, anticipate and expect a move of God and never doubt.

This book is a **"Prophetic Announcement"** to you of **"The Greatness of the Shift"** getting ready to be release to you and those faithfully serving even through their afflictions, hardships and the painful tests or trials. God has prophetically prepared a rebirth of the fivefold ministry gifts to the body to do what they were ordained to do by God from the beginning and that is to release nations into **"The Greatness of the Shift."** I hear a sound and stirring prophetically as God is raising up a great army like the Gideon Army to do great exploits. ***"But the people that do know their God shall be strong and do exploits"*** [Daniel 11:32b]. You can have confidence, complete confidence that God will keep His promises. The fulfillment of your Prophetic Destiny or Promise may not be the next day, but they will be *'in their own time'* on God's Divine Calendar.

Receive the Prophetic Messengers when they are sent by the Lord to announce your **"Supernatural Shift"** and don't be in a hurry to utter a word to anyone lest you abort it and be careful not to doubt the prophecy. The angel was a messenger from God name Gabriel sent to announce to Zacharias and Elizabeth their Supernatural Shift. A Shift means change, a change in your life to the glory of the Lord that cannot be denied. Gabriel is associated with the bearing of messages as revealed in Luke 1:26; and as also revealed in Daniel 8:16; 9:21.

The Angel response to Zacharias doubtful question about his shift. ***"Then the angel said, "I am Gabriel! I stand in the very presence of God. It was he who sent me to bring you this good news!"*** [Luke 1:19]. The prophet hears from God and speak for God. In those days God uses angels and prophets frequently to represent Him and carryout His assignments. This is still evident to today in the supernatural move of God under an Open Heaven in the kingdom that angelic visitations and supernatural release is happening globally as a remnant is responding to this clarion call, **"The Greatness of the Shift."** The angel explained that he himself was sign enough for Zacharias. ***"I am Gabriel,"*** he said, ***"I stand in the very presence of God."***

You will know and see the awe of God manifest, as these chosen Prophetic **"Carriers**

of the Shift" are sent on assignment to prepare you for your **"Greatness of the Shift,"** they will be soaked in the anointing. The Shift Anointing will be distinct as they stand in the very presence of God. Gabriel was sent to Zacharias with an extremely important message and Gabriel himself described it as good news. Gabriel the angel name means, *"Man of God."* As the angel promised, Elizabeth became pregnant.

If you are waiting on God for the fulfillment of a Prophetic Promise, or answer to a requestor to fulfill some need, I encourage you to keep calm and remain patient. No matter, how much medically impossible, economically impossible, financially impossible or naturally impossible it may appear, God made a promise to you and what he said in His word will come true, right on time. **"The Greatness of the Shift"** is God's Divine Hand released right on time. When God promises you, healing, breakthrough, and miraculous deliverance it will come true right on time.

Chapter 7

Get in the Shift

"Shift" means to move from one place to another. In this case the Lord desire for you is to come up higher. The Lord is saying, ***"Call unto me, and I will answer you, and show you great and mighty things, which you know not"*** [Jeremiah 33:3]. The **"Shift"** means to change emphasis or direction. God is about to bring about a change in your life suddenly. For some the **"Shift"** is just a slight change. We have seen throughout the Bible several shifts taking place in many great men or women lives. Many of these great men and women had favorable Shifts but there are few unfavorable ones such as when Saul lost his Kingly position out of disobedience. This is the same account of the first man or woman in the Bible, Adam and Eve who held the **'Key'** to the **"Shift"** and had Royal Access to the fullness of their inheritance as lost it because of deception through the serpent.

There were unfavorable shifts when the older generation of the Israelites did not make it into the promise because they were stiff-necked. On the other hand, there are several great men and women in the Bible whose lives were initially marked by unfavorable circumstances, but then suddenly what seems to be an unfavorable moment in their lives is what catapult them into Greatness. To enter all that God has for promised you must be willing to obey and walk by faith, not by sight. **"Get into the Shift"** is implying or indicating that you are prepared or have an idea. It is implying that you understand and have been given access. Get into the Shift is saying that you are ready to conceive and enter the change or transition God has predestined for your life. The only way into **"The Greatness of the Shift"** is by walking by faith. Obedience is not a Gift, if it was it would be very difficult to obtain for many in the Kingdom. Obedience is your willingness to accept what God says, and step into it without resistance, hesitation or rebellion.

Change is inevitable in our lives. Change takes hard work and you must be willing to make the sacrifice to get the rewards or benefits of change.

- **"The Greatness of the Shift"** is all about change, it sells new blessings, new connections, increase and unexpected miracles.
- **"The Greatness of the Shift"** is when God is getting ready to birth something awesome inside of you and through you.
- **"The Greatness of the Shift"** is a Season of Change from one dimension to another.
- **"The Greatness of the Shift"** is a season of enlargement and expansion in the Lord.

To achieve a positive change it takes consistent, tireless effort and dedication regardless of the challenges, trials or hindrances that comes with the territory or position you are called to operate in the Kingdom or the position you hold as a wife, mother, or just a citizen of the Kingdom. Being a part of the Kingdom, your impact is not limited to just the pulpit ministry, it could be you are an Educator or Teacher, a Cab Driver, mother, a wife, husband, choir member or even the janitor for the church. The idea is that **"Kingdom Shifters"** are called to be Pioneers or Catalyst for Change. Pioneers or Catalyst for Change [**Kingdom Shifters**] are a people who refuse to die. **"The Greatness of the SHIFT"** is experienced by a people who are convinced and confident that God is a promise keeper and that He is faithful to fulfill and bring to pass that which he purposed to do for those who trust Him and hope in His word.

"Get in the Shift" is marked by the assurance that, the Lord will perform that which He promised. God said in Exodus 34:20 ***"I will perform great wonders that I have not done anywhere before in all the earth."*** Eyes haven't seen, ears haven't heard the kind of blessings that is about to be released to you from the Lord. People will see what great things your God can do. God will do a new thing in you. He desires to do something awesome in your life. Something astounding, remarkable, overwhelming or breathtaking. Just the opposite of ordinary, God wants to do something extraordinary in your life. You may have seen God's favor in your life in the past. But God wants to release His unprecedented favor on you. Something that you have never known or experienced before, just like He did for Elizabeth and Zacharias.

Tipping Point

Your tipping point is your boiling point or breaking point. Everything that happens in your life builds a ladder to take you into your next level of Breakthrough. The Greatness of the SHIFT pushes you and makes you ascend. The place where you are shifted to ASCEND is called "Tipping Point" is a place of transition. It is a Breaking Point or Boiling Point. It indicates that something is SHIFTING or boiling over or breaking through. I believe in the Book of 1 Chronicles 4:9, Jabez was at this point, where he desperately needed to feel and see the manifestation of something greater than what he had suffered not just growing up, or during his manhood but from the painful conception from his mother's womb. Not to mention, the pain was a mark upon him even at birth.

> ***"There was a man named Jabez who was more honorable than any of his brothers. His mother named him Jabez* because his birth had been so painful. 10 He was the one who prayed to the God of Israel, "Oh, that you would bless me and expand my territory! Please be with me in all that I do and keep me from all trouble and pain!" And God granted him his request"***
> [1 Chronicles 4:9-10].

His birth was marked by pain or sorry, hence the reason why he was named Jabez. But it was the pain that provoke him to PUSH. I implore you from Jabez life and my own personal life testimonies and live changing experiences to **"PUSH, Don't Abort your Purpose, Destiny is Calling you,"** into **"The Greatness of the Shift."** Your warfare or pain is an indicator that "Greater is Coming." The Greatness of the Shift" is marked by pain, suffering, setbacks, rejection, disappointments and even betrayal, but you must PUSH, into **"The Greatness of the SHIFT."** In the natural birth of a child, the pain is the initial sign of a child getting ready to be born. The mother must endure that travail, groaning, bearing down and push beyond the pain she feels until she heard a cry from her baby symbolizing the manifestation, that he baby is alive and breathing in and air into the new place or environment called earth. Likewise, your painful trials or suffering is an indication that something new, something greater is getting ready to be birth out or manifest in your life.

What God has instore for you, just believe and be confident that God trust you to bear it. **"You are Anointed for This."** When your painful trial intensifies like Jabez or your warfare intensify with sickness, betrayal, setbacks, hard trials or disappointments, jealousy or opposition it is an indication that something big and beautiful is about to come forth in your life. When you feel like your back is against the wall and look like it is over, it is your **"Tipping Point"** into **"The Greatness of the SHIFT, Don't Abort Your Purpose Destiny is Calling You."** Job's warfare intensified when some of his friends or confidant were not to be found. Some may have misunderstood or misjudged your situation, but God had a plan.

God will get the glory out of your story. When I was facing a painful journey in my life, those I thought would be there or understand my situation turn their back on me. My late husband took very ill and I was not able to travel and minister. At the time when he took very ill it was in January 2012, one month after my Apostleship consecration in the bitter winter cold with five 5-year-old triplets to put on the school bus every morning and a (three) 3-year-old to also attend to. He was admitted in hospital an hour away from home. How did I balance that? It was very difficult. My parents lived with me at the time, but my dad would be at work as early as 4 am in the morning. So of course, my children would miss school some days or I would have to wait until they get on the bus to journey to the hospital some days.

It was a lonely place as a mother, wife and minister of the Gospel. I felt hurt and let down by those who I revered in ministry and I ask God why? Why would He allow these people to walk in my life and then turn their back when I needed them most. I really was at a place I called suffering in silence. It was then in that dark place that God was preparing me for my **"Greatness of the Shift."** Oh Yes, I was so disappointment and shocked, but I realize religion can keep you bound in rituals and church routine but a true relationship with Christ helps you to understand the power of His love. The Power of God loves can take you from a low place into a broad place suddenly. I had to let go and let God. It was in this place of silence is when I understood that, those who have done their time in your life will need to exit naturally and physically whether you like it or not.

Each time you feel like you are knocked down your perseverance will take you into **"The Greatness of the SHIFT"** into a place that you have never been before in the Lord. **"The Greatness of the SHIFT"** will take you into a realm of glory that you have never experienced before. What you are going through right now doesn't determine what's next for **'YOUR NEXT IS BETTER THAN NOW.'** **"The Greatness of the Shift"** encompasses the DNA of your Destiny. Every moment in your life is a deposit from God that will birth out something significant that you will remember, and these moments carries the DNA of your Destiny. Every painful experience, even if your mother was a victim of rape, even if your parents died or you were abandoned by your father or mother. God will use it to birth out your Prophetic Promise or Prophetic Destiny.

Prophetic Reset

While you are waiting on your release what have you done with your time. You must use your time wisely. Despite the challenges you must superimpose Romans 8:28 that, ***"all this work together for good."*** You must have a mindset that only good will come out of this. The sickness of my late husband in 2012 was what God used to birth out my first book, entitled, **"Awake to Your Destiny" Volume 1, "The Mind of Christ."** This was published on in Kindle Book Format three (3) after he was admitted in the hospital. The Lord used the situation I was in that was challenging and losing time outside the hospital to do other things to birth out the **"Awake to Your Destiny."** Right by his hospital bed I began to write this book for over three (3) weeks, as the Lord helped me to understand that, he allowed or permitted the challenges I was facing, the rejection or hurt from those who turned their backs on me.

The Lord is saying, *"don't be mad at them, understand this, that if they stay you will not be able to* **"Awake to Your Destiny**.*"* *"Where you are going man cannot take you there." "I will take you there." "People are only my instruments used to carry out my purposes in the earth. I the Lord of Host, I Am the Author of the Shift."*

When God says there is a **"Prophetic Reset"** of the promises in your life it means that something came to disrupt the flow of blessings or God's divine direction for your life. Because of this disruption by the enemy the Lord said I will reset everything. Reset means to move, reorder or reposition. It also means bringing back everything to its original position or intent. Naomi's life was interrupted by the death of her husband, and two sons. Ten (10) years later, the homeland she left to settle in Moab was now experiencing drought. She heard news that the Lord visited her homeland Bethlehem Judah, so she returned by faith into a life of new beginning.

God repositioned Naomi so that Ruth could come into **"The Greatness of the Shift."** The Prophetic Reset in our lives is divinely
orchestrated by the Lord to repositioned us to be blessed. Naomi's obedience to move **["SHIFT"]** from Moab to Bethlehem Judah also repositioned her daughter in law Ruth who went along with her. Ruth entered the fullness of her destiny because Naomi was sensitive to the Spirit of the Lord timing and release of **"Greatness of the Shift."** Ruth on arrival to Naomi's homeland wandered into the field of Boaz to glean after the reapers [Ruth Chapter 2]. Boaz the moment he laid eyes on her, there was a divine connection, he watched over her and Ruth found favor with Boaz. Boaz also gave instructions for her to be cared for by the men in the field and he told her not to go in any other field to glean. Ruth Chapter 4 reveals that Boaz married Ruth and they both became King-David

Great-Grandparents the lineage of our Lord and Savior Jesus Christ.

> *"My prayer is that you will be very sensitive to the times and seasons on God's Prophetic Calendar, so you will know that God is rearranging and repositioning you to be blessed. I pray you will obey His voice not your current situation and move in the direction the Lord is leading you into. I pray that you will collide with your divine soul mate and destiny helpers for your life, ministry or business. I pray that when your divine soul mate or destiny helpers lay eyes on you or connect with you that you will find favor in their eyes in Jesus name."*

When the Lord **"Prophetically Reset"** your life, those who are not a part of your destiny will not understand or be sensitive to the shift in your life. Oprah was not sensitive to the **"Greatness of the Shift."** It seems as if Oprah could not let go of her history. It seems she was still focus on the life in Moab where her ancestors worshipped other gods and possibly refuse to move from a place of mourning her husband Naomi's son.

> ***"Remember ye not the former things, neither consider the things of old.***
> ***19 Behold, I will do a new thing; now it shall spring forth; shall ye not know it?"*** [Isaiah 43:18-19].

Those who have turned their backs on you, who misunderstood you and separated themselves from you were not a part of your ultimate destiny. They have done their time or season in your life and now it's your time to "SHIFT" into greater. Those who are a part of the fullness of your destiny will stick and stay just like Ruth by God's divine plan. If they are not, they will turn back from following you.

Understand this, the supernaturally God transport you into **"The Greatness of the Shift"** for your life which also comes with separation from things and people who are not meant to be a part of what's next in your life. Where you are going, they are not a part of your Destiny, but the history. The things you go through as life changing trials and hardship, loss or disappointment is the history God will use to propel you into your Destiny. Two vital pieces to connect you to your **"Prophetic Reset"** for the **"Greatness of the Shift"** is your obedience and sensitivity to the Holy Spirit.

The Threshing Floor Experience

Jabez history was what pushed him to what I can only describe as the **"Threshing Floor Experience"** where the only focus is a desperation and passion for something new, for something greater. The **"Threshing Floor"** is a place where dreams and visions not only become clearer, but you get results. There is a visible or tangible manifestation that is activated because you were willing to pay the price. Like Jabez, you must be willing to see an opportunity in the middle of a crisis. Jabez used the setback, stigma to his name, labelled pain as an opportunity to seek the face of the Lord for **"Prophetic Reset."**

"The Greatness of the Shift" is a moment you can't afford to miscalculate our miss. The Bible said he was more honorable than his brethren that surrounded him. He didn't fit in and based on the information given in only two verses you gather that they already classified him as hopeless, not much room for change for Jabez in their mind because circumstances in his life has a history and stigma with pain. Isaiah 61:7 reassures us that: **"For your shame ye shall have double; and for**

confusion they shall rejoice in their portion:"

> *"I prophecy to you that your pain will make you known to the world. Your painful story or history will generate a global impact with signs and wonders to follow. I prophecy to you that, your testimony of how you made it over and came through your stormy trials shall release you into the Prophetic Whirlwind of God's favor."*

Don't just exist in time, use time to create opportunities that are without borders and limitations. Jabez stood in the gates with his brethren.

> **"And Jabez was more honourable than his brethren: and his mother called his name Jabez, saying, Because I bare him with sorrow"** [1 Chronicles 4:9]

His name meant distress and pain, yet the Bible said He was more honorable than his brothers. This indicates to me that what God speaks over your life is more powerful than any curse ever written against your name or against your life.

All God is waiting on is for you to "**Leap into Your Destiny**." The Book of 1 Chronicles 4 reveals in the first few verses a history of the descendants of the tribe of Judah, and after listing a few early in history of this tribe it just suddenly leaped over in verse 9 to talk about Jabez.

As a researched the Tribe of Judah history reveals that, during the time of the judges, the tribe of Judah was still isolated. In the great battle against Sisera, Judah is not even mentioned (Judges 5). But the tribe's isolation was ended after several Philistine invasions from the West, and especially after David captured Jerusalem and made it Judah's capital. Although in Judges 15:11 the men of Judah are prepared to hand over Samson to the Philistines, everything changed during the time when Samuel was judge. The ark was returned to Judah and lost territory was regained (1 Samuel 7:1). The Lord restored and reset the ark in Judah.

I use these facts to speak into your life **"Prophetic Reset"** that a great SHIFT is about to take place in your life suddenly, where everything will change, the presence of the Lord will be restored in your life in greater dimensions and magnitude. I prophecy to you that lost territory (land, blessings, promotion, elevation) shall be regain in the name of Jesus. I decree and declare Prophetic Reset over your life, you will rejoice and be glad. It was during the time of Samuel that these things were restored to Judah. Well, I prophecy to you that a Samuel Anointing and a Jabez Anointing of Divine Release is yours now, for you to regain all that you have lost, and you shall be completely restored physically, emotionally, mentally, spiritually and financially.

If Jabez and Samuel was from this tribe look what they have in common, their mother birth them out of a painful experience. Hannah was highly favored by her husband who offered her a worthier portion of the sacrifice than Peninnah his other wife. Yet she suffered great pain because of the ridicule from her adversary Peninnah who constantly reminded her she was barren and could not bear a child. But Peninnah forget, it was the Lord that shut up Hannah's womb. Shout it out Lord, MY COME BACK IS GREATER! I'm getting ready for **"The GREATNESS OF THE SHIFT!"** To those who tried to rob you of your dignity, respect, self-worth and confidence what God is about to do in your life will silence them forever. Samuel birth created a global impact. When you

"Persevere, Until the, Shifts, Happen [P.U.S.H.]" what the Lord birth out of the womb of your destiny shall speak volume and impact the lives of those around you positively. For some the Lord will change your story like Hannah to be known or visible on the global platforms that the Lord will position you that His name will be Glorified.

My pain and suffering in the sickness and unexpected death of my late husband was what the Lord used to birth out **"The Greatness of the Shift"** in my life. By November 2015 I released my third book series that was already copyrighted from December 2014 entitled, **"I Am Anointed for This - Prophetic Unlocking"** *Declaring War for Your Destiny through Power Charge Prophetic Nuggets and Prophetic Prayer Declaration."*

Don't let your suffering, or pain be an excuse to remain stagnant or immobile. Don't allow the ridicule, insults, jealousies or rejection from men become an hinderance to you stepping into greatness and leaping into your destiny. Get up and use these negative arrows against you to **"P.U.S.H, [*Persevere, Until the, Shifts, Happen*], Don't Abort Your Purpose Destiny is Calling You."** It was a familiar ground for Jabez and it was a familiar ground for Hannah, where every day they wake up expecting the same thing to happen, pain and ridicule. Constantly being reminded of their barrenness and pain by the way they were treated. But I realize that though 1 Chronicles 4:9-10 only reveals one prayer request prayed by Jabez I don't believe it was his first and last prayer. I believe overtime he was persistent in his prayers and this was a **"Tipping Point"** prayer that propelled him into a great shift.

The cycles that you want broken shall be broken and destroyed by the anointing and power from your very own mouth. **"The Greatness of the Shift,"** your defining moment of change is coming out of your mouth. It's time to arise and prophecy over your life. For out of your belly shall flow rivers of living waters!!! I double dare you right now to begin to cry out, and prophecy out loud 1 Chronicles 4:10 below three (3) times until you feel a SHIFT,

> *"Oh, that you would bless me and expand my territory! Please be with me in all that I do and keep me from all trouble and pain!"*

"Don't Abort your Purpose, Destiny is Calling You." Get ready for **"The Greatness of**

the Shift" *for the ground beneath you may seem familiar but what God is releasing to you shall be initiated through the realm of the supernatural.*

"Prophetic Reset" is the **"Suddenlies of God"** being activated in your life where everything can change instantly by the Power of the Holy Spirit that will be life changing to you and many will emerge and become **"Carriers of the Anointing of the Shift"** helping others come into what God has instore for them. Sometimes you may feel like you want to let go, but the **"Greatness of the Shift"** requires perseverance. That is to keep moving, keep doing, keep focus looking straight ahead for "What's coming is GREATER than what it's been.

Greater comes with a price. When God is taking you into *"Greatness"* expect opposition, persecution, trials and attacks to come, but let nothing separate you from the love of God which is in Christ Jesus our Lord and Savior. In **"The Greatness of the Shift"** God will raise you up to bring deliverance to the same ones who left you for dead, who talked about you and misunderstood you and what you were going through. You are coming out perfect. Moreover, what didn't kill you is getting ready to promote you.

I decree and declare that your later will be greater than the former. It is a new season coming to you and for sure you will testify like Job, **"For I've heard rumors about you, but now my eyes have seen you."**

Chapter 8

KINGDOM BUSTED TO P.U.S.H

Testimony of the Miraculous Birth of My Children

From the story in the book of 1 Samuel 1 Hannah's life was marked by barrenness, yet year after year journeying to Shiloh her tenacity was astounding as she remained faithful in worship and faith. Her tenacity shifted her from **"Barrenness into Greatness."** She constantly pursued and chased after God. Hannah was desperate for a **"Shift"** [change] in her life and she was willing to pay the price by presenting herself as a living sacrifice. Hannah also brought tangible sacrifices to the altar of the Lord. She wept sore before the Lord many times, but one day in Shiloh thing were about to shift suddenly.

"The Greatness of the Shift" is birthed out of a spirit of expectancy and perseverance. Show me someone who has tenacity and I will show you someone who is a candidate for a miracle. Perseverance is the breathing ground for a miracle. It was the spirit of expectancy and perseverance that birthed the **"The Suddenlies of God"** into Hannah's life. **"The Greatness of the Shift"** in your life must be marked by the spirit of expectancy and tenacity.

Has God ever made you a promise to you at a time or season when it seems like the odds were against it? Well this is my story of the **"Suddenlies of God"** miracles in my life. What I want to share with you briefly is the miraculous birth of my children when the odds were against me.

I was married to the late Pastor Richard Manning on December 18, 1999. When we got married Richard was already living in the United States of America where he migrated shortly after we met in Bible College, we had a brief courtship after we met in 1997 then he went away in April 1997 and returned for our wedding and honeymoon in December 1999. We remain apart for approximately three (3) years due to immigration proceedings. We only saw each other once per year. One of those years he couldn't make it to Jamaica because being married and living apart he had to make certain sacrifices for his health due to nose bleeds riding a bike daily to work in the snow time. So, we agreed he would save his airfare as a deposit towards a vehicle.

Miraculously that same year being the third year my immigration paper work was finally being processed in August the month he would generally visit Jamaica on vacation. He wasted no time, after my interview process was complete and passport stamped by the United States of America Embassy. He booked me a one-way ticket to New Jersey. I migrated September 2003 with the joyous intentions to begin a family. I wanted to have children desperately and decided I would begin to work on it right away. Oh yes, I was not going to waste any time. We intended to do what all married folk enjoy making babies happen. I know any woman in my position instinct would be the same, that is to make up for lost time and enjoy the blessedness of intimacy in marriage.

I got pregnant within in a few months after I migrated. Then unfortunately, I had a miscarriage in April of the following year 2004. I was eight (8) weeks pregnant, and upon doing the ultrasound it reveals that there was no pulse and the ultrasound was reflecting the size of a six (6) week old in the womb. I was placed under anesthesia and the fetus was removed. It was a painful experience. But the Lord gave me one scripture after I woke up, that is Isaiah 61:7 **"For your shame you shall possess the double."** I am here to tell someone, in my Apostolic and Prophetic Voice when it seems like your dream has died dream again.

The late Deaconess Norma Hudson, who stood in agreement with me that the laws of United States of America would change from five years to three years for the immigration filing process for married couples. We met the criteria for this law because of the year he submitted the application which afforded me the opportunity to live and work in America until my immigration process was complete. Deaconess Hudson stood in agreement with me for this law to be passed in the United States also told me before I migrate that God says, **"I will make all things beautiful in its time."** Yes, God did it in His time. In the time when it was on His Divine Calendar.

It was after two (2) miscarriages that my Suddenly of God miracles manifested. When the light shine in darkness, darkness shall not overcome it, that summarize basically **"The Greatness of the SHIFT." Kingdom Busted** means that out of your darkness of despair, trials, afflictions, persecution, rejection or pain

God uses it to unlock the treasures within you. Kingdom Busted means our dreams and visions are birth out of darkness – ***"The Thick Darkness."*** Understand, that in the History of the Bible from Genesis we see that in the thick darkness: - that's where God was. Genesis 1:1-2 says,

> ***"In the beginning God created the heavens and the earth. 2 The earth was formless and empty, and darkness covered the deep waters. And the Spirit of God was hovering over the surface of the waters."***

When you go through dark times or moments in your life don't make cheap talk about it. It is time to move deeper and get beyond the dim view and superficial talks about the history of the Bible and declare in confidence that: *"The darkness of my despair, painful trials and circumstances is where God was and is." His light shines in my darkness and the darkness cannot put it out. I decree and declare that, "The darkness cannot put out the light of God."*

Coupled with Divine Revelation from the Holy Spirit, my own personal experience and testimony, this book, **"The Greatness of the Shift"** encourages you to **P.U.S.H. [Persevere Until Something Happens]**. It was designed to empower and encourage you to ***"Don't Abort Your Purpose, Destiny Is Calling You."*** The book of Habakkuk 2:3 declares,

> ***"This vision is for a future time. It describes the end, and it will be fulfilled. If it seems slow in coming, wait patiently, for it will surely take place. It will not be delayed."***

Whatever is standing in the way of your deliverance or breakthrough shall bow, must bow to the name of Jesus. At times we ask the question like Habakkuk:

- How long shall this evil prevail against my marriage?
- How long shall this evil prevail against my finances?
- How long shall this evil prevail against my spiritual aspirations and or ministry?

- How long shall evil prevail against my relationship(s)?

The Power of Crying Out

Crying before God doesn't mean you are weak, He understand your tears, its release, its cleansing, it's the unloading your thoughts, and feelings to God that cannot be explained with words. When you cry unto God, He arise to help you. You are not weak as men think or even you may think of yourself. I weep a lot in prayer, and many don't understand that and why. Psalm 61 says, **"Hear my cry oh Lord, attend unto my prayer. From the ends of the earth will I cry unto thee."** Well, my cry initially after migrating and attempting to conceive was, **"How long shall evil prevail, Lord help me I AM BARREN?"**

As mention the Lord spoke to me a Prophetic Promise, double for my trouble from Isaiah 61:7. Habakkuk 2:3 affirms this promise as well. Therefore, God responds to you just like He responded to me and to Habakkuk saying even though His response **"Seemed slow in coming, wait patiently, for it will surely take place. It will not be delayed."** The Lord spoke to Habakkuk in verse 2 and 3a, to write down what He said pertaining to the **"Greatness of the Shift,"** reassuring him that the vision was for a future time. It describes the end, and it will be fulfilled.

The future time indicted that it was already predetermined by God your breakthrough. Future time indicates it was already predetermined by God who you will marry. Future time means it was already predetermined when the blessings, dreams and aspiration will manifest according to Gods Divine Plan and Calendar for your life. This definition indicates that the future time for me to have children was on God's Calendar. I became impatient and tried to help God's hand move a little faster. In other words, I was trying to speed up the process. Which resulted in two (2) miscarriages.

The vision was for a future time Habakkuk 2:3a revealed. The pain you are experiencing now, or suffering may seem unbearable but the beauty of your test or trial produced from waiting and enduring hard trials will manifest. Your trial or test will be used to propel you into your promise. It was very painful when I lost my babies to miscarriage, but I had to bring to remembrance the Prophetic Promise the Lord gave to us. When God speaks a word of promise to us, He does not repent of His promise. The Lord watches over His word to perform it. Isaiah 46:11b affirms it, **"Yea, I have spoken it, I will also bring it to pass; I have purposed it, I will also do it."**

Just as Habakkuk was encouraged to wait patiently for God's Divine hand of judgement to be released against evil, this book is to encourage you and strengthen. you that, the vision is yet for an appointed time. God is releasing this word of assurance to you that, although the fulfillment will not take place for a while, the fact that God said it should be cause enough to maintain faith.

> **"It is good that a man should both hope and quietly wait for the salvation of the LORD"** [Lamentations 3:26].

This means to patiently bear affliction, waiting for God to act and to accept his will even in suffering. In Jeremiah's darkest moment, his hope was strengthened with this assurance: God had been faithful and would continue to be faithful.

In my darkest moment the scripture verses God gave me as a seal and sign of His promise that I would have a child was from Isaiah 61:7 that, **"for your (my) shame you (I) shall**

possess the double." It gave me hope and assurance. I believed the Lord. I held on to His love and comfort during that dark place of feeling sad over the miscarriages. I honestly did not lose hope because I believe God has been faithful and will continue to be faithful. The **"Greatness of the Shift"** was made manifest after two miscarriages. The second miscarriage I received the same promise from God, Isaiah 61:7, but I was also instructed by God to not only pray but also increase my level of prayers of thanksgiving and praise.

Through the divine revelations that I received and believed from the Lord to intensify my praise and worship it saturated my uterus and made it fertile naturally and spiritually for God to activate the seeds for my miracle. Praise is the birthing position for a miracles. If you are not an avid praiser get started and position yourself for a miracle. My husband also received a revelation from the Lord that before the seed was even formed within me to conceive, the enemy tried to kill it. He said the Lord told him to tell me somethings only go by prayer and fasting. I listened keenly to the words of encouragement from the Lord and the divine Instructions given to me and maintain vigilance in fasting, prayer and praise.

I cried a lot during the second miscarriage. Cooking, washing or just resting I was crying or weeping. The second week after my second miscarriage my late husband laid hands and prayed. He said this was not normal nor healthy because it is a sign of a breakdown or decline emotionally which can lead to depression, stress or anxiety. He laid hands on me and prophesied Isaiah 61:3: -

"To console those who mourn in Zion, to give them beauty for ashes, The oil of joy for mourning, The garment of praise for the spirit of heaviness;"

As He prophesied over me these verses something supernatural happen in my mind, body, soul and spirit. These verses given to me by God and released by my husband cushion and propelled me to **P.U.S.H. [Persevere Until the SHIFT Happens].** I was Kingdom Busted to unlock the GREATNESS within from a very dark place, suffering from two (2) miscarriages because I believe and received the revelation given to me to strengthen me and heal me. Are you looking back only on your past to form negative opinions about your situation? Or are you meditating on God's word or promises to uplift your spirit and propel you forward. God uses the darkness as a pivotal point for the creation of the universe. Likewise, He will also use our dark period of suffering, test and trials to bring forth or manifest the Kingdom of God from within us.

The Kingdom of God is established for us to be **"fruitful and multiply; fill the earth and subdue it; have dominion..."** [Genesis 1:28]. I prophecy to you that you have been Kingdom Busted by God to **"fruitful and multiply; fill the earth and subdue it; have dominion..."** for out of your trouble on every side, afflictions and painful test and trials God will use it to induce spiritual labor. In the labor room, women wail, cry out and push as they feel the contraction pain and the baby pushing against their cervix canal. God has taken you into a dark place not to destroy you but rather for you to persevere and trust Him in the darkness until the light overtake it and the excellency of His power unlocks the treasures in your earthen vessel.

> **"But we have this treasure in earthen vessels, that the excellency of the power may be of God, and not of us"** [2 Corinthians 4:7].

God is using every troubling situation, everything that comes to perplex you, the persecution or hard-pressed trials to cultivate, birth out and bring out the treasures that lies within you. The weapon that was formed against you shall not prosper. It was meant for evil, but God is using it for your greater good. You have been **"Kingdom Busted."**

Jabez remained faithful even in difficult times. The Bible says he was more honorable than his brothers. Honorable means admiral, moral, and descent. It also means righteous, honest truthful, dependable and good. Despite his dark place of pain, and stagnation emotionally that crippled his destiny psychologically, geographically and physiological God saw him maintaining an honorable life before Him, one of righteousness, reputable and honest.

> Psalm 4:3 says ***"But know that the Lord hath, set apart those that are godly for Himself; the Lord will hear when I call unto him."***

Jabez was named by His mother aligning His destiny with distress and pain. She said, **"Because I bare him with sorrow"** [1 Chronicles 4:9b]. Jabez carried that history of pain for many years and not only was He labelled distress or pain because his mother called him Jabez but based on the History of the text Canaan was facing war with other nations. He was now an honorable man possibly was representing His country and desired to see the SHIFT [change] manifest in the land. As an honorable man he carried within his loins the anointing to shift kingdoms or nations into alignment by maintaining his faith and trust in the living God. You are called and destined to be a **"Carrier of the Shift"** anointing not just for your release, but for your family and the nations the Lord has given you as a strategical place to live or as a Kingdom Assignment.

Many are faced with challenges not just financially, emotionally or physically but also spiritual warfare. The Lord is provoking you in this chapter to take on the spiritual positioning of Jabez to overcome every darkness by crying out with tenacity and fervency decreeing and declaring:

> ***"Oh, that thou wouldest bless me indeed, and enlarge my coast, and that thine hand might be with me, and that thou wouldest keep me from evil, that it may not grieve me!"*** [1 Chronicles 4:9].

After Jabez **P.U.S.H** [Persevered Until the SHIFT Happens] with expectancy there was a manifestation**, *"And God granted him that which he requested"*** [1 Chronicles 4:9b]. Your darkness whatever your case, may it provoke you like Jabez to **"P.U.S.H** [Persevere Until the Shift Happens]**, Don't Abort your Purpose Destiny is Calling You into "The Greatness of the Shift."**

Chapter 9

Kingdom Shifters

This is the season that God is releasing to the body of Christ supernatural revelation to Win. This is the season that God is raising up **"Kingdom Shifters." "Kingdom Shifters"** are men and women that have experience great devastation or sufferings in their life that men would use to disqualify them but in turn God use it to qualify them to become. Carriers of the **"SHIFT." "Kingdom Shifters"** are those that have been in a dark place in their lives that seem hopeless as if there is no way out but by the Divine Hand of God you have come back to life fortified with the word of God and **"Empowered to WIN." "Kingdom Shifters"** have been **"Restored to Win"** and repositioned by God to own their success.

- As a **"Kingdom Shifter"** you own your success. As a **"Kingdom Shifter"** you must own your breakthrough.
- As a Kingdom Shifter you must own your miracle.

- As a Kingdom Shifter you must position yourself with a spirit of expectancy for the ***"Greatness of the Shift."***

The greatest supernatural move of God is birthed through men and women considered by others as not worthy, not qualified for the call, purpose or position. But in God's eyes they are not qualified for the call, purpose or position as **"Kingdom Shifters."** This is your season of discovery as God is seeking out those that are being overlooked to be discovered.
- Is it you, the very ones seen as an outcast, despised and rejected by men?
- Have you experience public shame in your life or ministry?
- Have you been labeled an outcast on the job, in your family or even within the church community?
- Were you told by the doctor that your situation will not change except you receive a Divine Miracle?
- Were you the one your parents told you that they tried to abort, or they almost miscarried you during the pregnancy?
- Have you been suffering from mental fatigue and depression, because everything

you tried to do in life it seems like it has failed?
- Are you the one they have talked about in a negative manner because of the false accusations and lies they heard about your life or situation?
- Do you feel like Jeremiah, not competent or don't have what it takes even though the call is evident, and you have received several confirmations?
- Do you feel like Joseph that because of your dream you are despised and hated by your biological and spiritual brothers or sisters?

> *"I declare to you that a God is about to change your story and he alone will get the glory. God is getting you ready for a Supernatural Visitation, Divine Shift and He will use every painful trial and suffering you have been through as an opportunity for you to manifest signs and wonders. You are a Kingdom Shifter.*

God has handpicked you to be Kingdom Busted for a dangerous deliverance like the four Lepers at the Gate that will propel you into the Suddenlies of God encounter changing your story and birthing within you the anointing to become a **"Carrier of the Shift."** Declare this out loud, *my situation is about to change, my story will change in Jesus name,* **"I Am A Kingdom Shifter."** Even though it seems like your purpose has caused others to doubt you, stand boldly to speak and declare Gods word. Stand boldly and leap into your purpose and destiny. Stand boldly and walk into the fullness of the dream or vision God has given to you. God will use your circumstances to show forth His Glory. He will ignite you with the His spirit power to move forward just as He did the four lepers at the gate to become a Kingdom Shifters. Be strong and remain focus on the assignment.

Your assignment could be to a man, or a woman, in marriage or personal relationships. Your assignment could be to your family, marriage, business sector, the market place, an intercessor, fivefold leader or a Global Ambassador for Christ. I implore you through these pages, don't be discouraged by troublemakers, like Sanballat and Tobias who delight in stirring people to controversy. Understand this, the Sanballat's and Tobias' are trying to distract you and plotting to overthrow you. But I have news for you while they are plotting to over throw your Destiny, while they are trying to hinder your release or supernatural breakthrough God shall overthrow them and make your dream greater. Shout Glory!!! I'm getting ready to see something I've never seen.

I encourage you to maintain your position by standing on God's word for the GREATNESS OF THE SHIFT shall manifest suddenly. For, when it looks like death that's when Jesus inevitably steps in. Know this, God cannot work with any sacrifice that's not willing to be crucified, crushed, beaten or pressed. You must be willing to experience the process as a death experience. A true servant, son or daughter of God must be willing to die first, to forsake your own ideologies, rational, personal agenda or fleshly lust and desires to experience **"The Greatness of the Shift."** God releases his Glory from a dark place. God releases His glory in our lives when we are apparently in a dangerous place. We look to watch action movies on television or in the cinema right, but we cannot endure our own transition from darkness or danger into a greater deliverance prophetically called by God as **"The Greatness of the Shift."** It's called *"Dangerous Deliverance."*

A great shift in your life will follow a great trial or test. As we were discussing, the four lepers were at a very dark place in their lives. They were even considered dangerous to be around because of their disease. They were social outcast. The Book of Numbers Chapter 5 affirms this detail explicitly that someone with leprosy is a *"Ceremonially Unclean"* person is always isolated.

> **"And the LORD spoke to Moses, saying: 2 "Command the children of Israel that they put out of the camp every leper, everyone who has a discharge, and whoever becomes defiled by a corpse. 3 You shall put out both male and female; you shall put them outside the camp, that they may not defile their camps in the midst of which I dwell." 4 And the children of Israel did so, and put them outside the camp; as the LORD spoke to Moses, so the children of Israel did."**

> *I prophecy to you that you are a Carrier of the Shift Anointing to unlock dreams and visions that will not just be a blessing for your life. You are a Carrier of the Shift Anointing to help*

others tap into their untapped potential.

Because of your painful or devastating circumstances God has deposited in the **"DNA of your Destiny"** anointing to shift into greatness. It is remarkable to know that God chose you as a medium to get the message out to other believers and those who have lost hope to tell them, ***"Don't Die Here, Refuse to Die Here Be Ready to Shift."***

The Lepers at the gate not only experience **"The Greatness of the Shift"** supernatural encounter, they also could not keep it to themselves. After they experienced it and tasted it, they could not keep it to themselves. They saw from their leap of faith the dangerous deliverance of God that brought about great blessings and restoration all because they take the chance of plunging into the Syrians camp. They didn't keep it to themselves, they were willing to help others who were hungry for food and desperate for a breakthrough. The four leprous men, knowing that, there may be a chance we might die, but if we stay here, we may die also, so why not **SHIFT**, persevering rather than regressing they were blessed.

Instead of, remaining in a dead place at the gate, thy step out and step up and God caused the enemies to hear a noise and left the camp, so they could be experience **"The Greatness of the Shift."** After this supernatural encounter they decided this revelation and encounter we cannot keep it to ourselves.

> *"Then they said to one another, "We are not doing right. This day is a day of good news, and we remain silent. If we wait until morning light, some punishment will come upon us. Now therefore, come, let us go and tell the king's household"* [2 Kings 7:9].

I cannot keep it to myself either. Miracles still happen, and I am a living testimony that no matter how dead or dark your life situation seem God can deliver you unexpectedly. The Lord has anointed me to release this book to prophecy to someone's purpose and destiny that you were **"Born to be a Great."** The only way to experience greatness is with faith, passion and tenacity no matter what it looks like and matter how others misjudge, mistreat or criticize your situation. Be very careful how you judge another person dark place. Just because you don't understand it, or you raise judgement against it doesn't mean God is not in it or cannot work through it.

I had a doctor who mocked me when I was pregnant with my second child. One day from the twenty-one (21) weeks safe zone of the pregnancy I had my second miscarriage. The doctor mocked me each time I visit his office for a Prenatal checkup about my condition of fibroid. Yes, He would not tell me anything positive. During those visits, not one time did he tell me how my baby was doing. Instead, he kept confessing doom, *"oh Fibroid getting bigger."* Next visit same thing. My late husband and I were getting concerned that this doctor gave us no hope. Don't panic when mockers mock your dream. *"Don't Panic, Level Up"* when men condemn you and write you off as good for nothing.

You have the power to speak life to your deliverance or destiny. Proverbs 18:21 **"Death and life are in the power of the tongue: and they that love it shall eat the fruit thereof."** I come to prophecy to you, *"Confront the things that you are afraid of."* Inner satisfaction comes from true and good speech, **"Death and life:"** The words people say wield great power. God is all powerful and when He speaks, His words wield greater power. God's Words shall not return to Him void of Power. As a child of living we are designed to be carriers of that same Glory that what we speak shall be made manifest suddenly. We are **"Kingdom Shifters"** design to be **"Carriers of Shift."**

What this doctor did to us and meant for evil God worked it for my good. He didn't tell us how the baby was doing, and we decided we were going to address this in prayer and confront this next visit. But the damage was done that I found myself in excruciating pain at work, from not having enough fluid and rest contrary to what the Peninnah Spirit Doctor was implying that Fibroids was growing not my baby. When I called the doctor, he told me to go home and elevate my legs and rest. It was a Friday evening with no change, so I called back he said go to the emergency room near me. There are some people in your life giving you advise that seems good, but it leads to the road of defeat and destruction.

Proverbs 23:7b says, *"Eat and drink!" he says to you, but*
his heart is not with you."

Proverbs 27:6 *"Faithful are the wounds of a friend; but the*

kisses of an enemy are deceitful."

As I write this I am being translated into the supernatural realm where God is showing me that some of you have been seated at a table with men and women or both who expect you to fail not win. *But I prophecy to you today that you will not fail in no area of your life, you will win.* Continue to lift your eyes to the hills from whence cometh your help, you help cometh from the Lord according to Psalm 121, the God you serve cannot slumber, nor sleep. Even when the journey seems long and weary and you feel like giving up remember, on your journey into Destiny, your Promises Blessings, Healing or Breakthroughs God is never off duty, He is right there with you carrying you for he **"Neither slumbers nor sleep."**

I was living in Wildwood at the time but visiting a doctor an hour away because I was building a home in that area. New to the medical system in America, I did not know that he wasn't registered with that hospital to practice medicine or visit his patients. So, the Obstetrician who I was seeing when I lost my first (1st.) child was the one on call for duty that weekend in the emergency room where I was living. When he discovered it was me lying in the emergency room, he did not come in to see me but told the nurse and the attending doctor at 2:00 am in the morning to discharge me. I was in excruciating pain and the Attending Doctor and male nurse was very sympathetic but told me they were sorry with tears in their eyes. They were told by the Obstetrician on call to let me go home.

There are many who hear about your story and even my story and they cast doubts on your situation. You thought they would be there for you to encourage you and walk with you through this dark valley. This Dark Valley is just a shadow and an indication that you are getting Ready to Shift. My friends the Lord will give you the strength and courage to do things that you could not have done before. I prophetically announce to you that God's Grace and Mercy shall follow you this day and will overshadow you to come forth into the fullness of what He has in store for you.

See, the previous doctor didn't want to handle my issues. Not everyone can handle what you are about to manifest as greatness. Furthermore, some folk are Destiny Killers, Joy Killers, and Destiny Thieves. They come to hear your story to bring you lower not higher in God. The Obstetrician overseeing my then second pregnancy in 2004 not only spoke doom to me but he also gave me wrong advise and abandoned me. So, he thought that without him speaking life to my situation I cannot receive anything. I am here to testify my God can do anything and everything but fail. But there is a God who loves me, who wrapped me in his arms and told me things were going to get easier. Don't worry my child things were going to get brighter. At the time, I could not see it, but I held on to the promise.

Can I encourage you in this your new season, ask God who should be your closet confidant and close to you in this season? Why you may ask? Because some are appointed as midwives to help you give birth and there are some who are abortionist sent by Lucifer himself to kill your purpose, dreams or destiny. You can't change your story, but you can use your story as a tool for unlocking the Greatness within you.

I prophecy to you for **"For your shame you shall possess the double."** In less than 24 hours after they discharged me, I had a second miscarriage. My Father-in-Law took me to the hospital while my husband was busy trying to pick up the prescription at the pharmacist that Saturday afternoon. I was in the shower when I felt pressure in my cervix canal. I grabbed my house robe and put it on called on my father-in-law door who lived in next door. He rushed me to the emergency room. He left me in the Emergency Room Registrar Office Section in the wheel chair and left me to park. She attempted to go through the routine questioning. I tell you I was crying and in pain. I felt embarrassed, I tried to explain in excruciating pain what my father in law already told her that I'm having a miscarriage. She asked me for medical insurance card and I told her I was in their database already. She insisted not only for my name, but address. I repeatedly told the lady I am losing my baby.

I could feel the pain and pressure the more so I had to push my body all the way out in the chair because I was getting very uncomfortable from the pain and the pressure. She insisted on asking again for my name, address and so on. Graphically you can imagine what happens next. My hands pushed back on my robe and she saw exactly why I could not give her any details about due to the excruciating pain with the fetus coming down.

She screamed "nurse! nurse! *"frantically"* a couple times and the double door on the right swung open and they rushed me into the emergency room. I had to push out my dream that night one day shy of twenty one (21) weeks. My dream died a second time. It was a still born baby boy, that had everything fully formed and no breath in him. Nathan died. But I was encouraged by the Holy Spirit to dream again. I received a confirmation phone call from a dear friend Sharon White in Jamaica giving me the same scripture verse, **"But for your shame you shall possess the double."** God saw that I was tore up from the floor up but he gave me hope. I was devasted by the loss, crying profusely for several days. The Lord saw my promise lying dead before me a second time, but He knew this painful process will ultimately birth out greatness. The Greatness of the Shift that ultimately will take you into your Destiny, breakthrough, healing or deliverance is birth out out of a hard trial or painful experience or test. The scripture says that he will not cause you to be tempted beyond that which you can bear, but in every temptation, he would make a way of escape.

"Don't Panic– Look UP - For Defeat is Not an Option." There is a treasure in you, and in order for the oil to flow, from the olive there is a process of the shaking, beating and the pressing. Grapes cannot produce or release the juices from it unless they are crushed.

> ***"But we have this treasure in earthen vessels, that the excellency of the power may be of God, and not of us"*** [2 Corinthians 4:7].

Chapter 10

Don't Abort Your Purpose Destiny Is Calling You

The **"Greatness of the Shift"** may seems like an exciting or thrilling experience by the heading but it is really birth out of the painful life experiences, trials and setbacks you had to endure in your season of waiting. *"I decree and declare that your come back shall be greater than your setbacks."* Oh yes it shall be in the end. But the journey to get there is marked by painful survival.

The **"Greatness of the Shift"** reveals to you in all situations that you will not be denied your promise no matter what the trials God will see you through. for *"Defeat is not an Option"* When God makes a promise, He keeps His covenant. Your blessings may seem delayed, but it is not denied by God. When others try to mock your situation and make you feel as if God has forgotten you Don't Panic Look Up for Defeat is not an Option. Regardless of how long the journey seems, God shall turn your defeat into astounding, overwhelming victory. Don't Panic – Look Up and Be Ready to Shift.

I felt defeated and panicked for a moment until the nurse told me the next morning that, she recommends that I hold my still born baby before I got discharged. My late husband and I both wept as she left the room giving us time to think about it. I requested to hold Nathan. The nurse brought him into my room and held my baby close in my arms. I was then my journey to receive closure began. When I came face to face with what was already broken, it was then that I was able to move forward.

At times the horrible things that happens to us ends up being the most fundamental part of our personal growth. You must be able to deal with the things you cannot change, to move forward. **"Acceptance of what has happened is the first step to overcoming the consequences of any misfortune."** [William James]. We were in so much pain. We thought it was the doctor's fault, and it was. If only he would have done his job while treating me for UTI infection which was common in pregnancies, he did not instruct me or treatment me for that instead was focus on my history of fibroids. Even though, the natural the circumstances leading to the second

miscarriage could have been avoided if proper care was given my doctor. Despite what led to the second miscarriage I had to focus on the fact that the seasons in our lives comes with many changes and that the Lord was still in control despite the trauma and the pain.
"Getting over a painful experience is much like crossing monkey bars. You have to let go at some point in order to move forward."
– C.S. Lewis.

A Promise is A Promise

When faced with challenges or painful circumstances you need to focus on the author of times and seasons holding on to the promises of God without wavering for, He is faithful who promised. Isaiah 46:11b declares,

> ***"Yea, I have spoken it, I will also bring it to pass; I have purposed it, I will also do it."***
>
> ***"As surely as I have spoken, I'll make it happen. I have planned, and yes, I'll do it."***

A promise is a declaration that one will do or refrain from doing something specified. I love the following definition because it is so in the eye of the prophetic:

- A promise is a legal binding declaration that gives to whom it is made a right to expect or claim the performance a specified.

- A promise is a reason to expect something especially, it is a ground for expectation of success, improvement [manifestation] or excellence.

I'm leaping and jumping right now shouting hallelujah and agreeing with heaven for divine intervention on your behalf. By the definition given for **"A Promise"** it affirms that, you have a right to expect or claim God's blessings for your life. It also, says, you have a reason to expect it. A promise is by covenant with God that what He has spoken, [He] ***"will make it happen...,"*** [He] ***"has purposed it, He will also do it."*** When God promises something, He will do it. It will certainly happen.

Who would have thought it was possible with the doom of fibroids and constant UTI's to have triplets then two years later another child? My doctors last words to me after I went for a follow up visit from the miscarriage was *"even if it's possible there is a slim chance."* I told him I fasted and prayed for 3 days before I met with Him. I told him the God I serve is able, and I have faith to believe He will fulfill what he promised to me. He said well then, let me refer you to a genetics Doctor, they may be able to tell you why you keep losing your babies.

I took the referral because, God made a promise to us. During that painful season of multiple miscarriages was indeed my refining moment or process. Without the heating or melting during the refining process there could be no purifying. God must purify you for **"The Greatness of the Shift."** One thing is constant is that. God's presence is guaranteed in the refining process. You are being purified for Greatness. The Lord is with you during the purification process. God wants to be the reflection in our lives.

> ***"I will bring that group through the fire and make them pure. I will refine them like silver and purify them like gold. They will call on my name, and I will answer them.***
> ***I will say, 'These are my people,' and they will say, 'The Lord is our God"*** [Zechariah 13:9].

This group is a small part of the whole Israel population. It is a "third" meaning a remnant. A remnant is a small part of the whole. Throughout the history of Israel, whenever the whole nation seemed to turn against God, God always considered and preserved a remnant, that regardless of their afflictions and hard-pressed trial who still trusted and followed him. These righteous remnant [believers] were refined like silver and gold through the fire of their difficult circumstances. They are determined to be part of God's remnant, are proven by their fiery trials to become **"Kingdom Shifters"** who are God ordained and empowered to be carriers of **"The Greatness of the Shift."** That small part of the whole [Remnant] Kingdom Shifters that are obedient to him, walking in faith, obeying God no matter what the rest of the world does. As **"Kingdom Shifters,"** this may mean trials and troubles at times; But as fire purifies gold and silver, you will be purified and made more like Christ to impact to nations.

In all honesty immediately after I migrated here to the United States of America, I was trying to rush the process of making babies. My husband and I were apart for three years due to the immigration process, so I was excited and very anxious to make babies happen. I did not want to waste any more time. So, I insisted as I told the woman of God Deaconess Hudson, after she gave me the prophetic word that I was going to work on babies as soon as I migrate. I can recall she laughed and said, take up that one with God because, I just deliver the word, *"He will make all things beautiful in its time."* She never lived to see the babies when they were born. But she helped me stay focus and strong in prayer until her passing.

I knew God was merciful to me by giving me another chance to be broken and blessed. You cannot enter **"The Greatness of the Shift"** without a Divine Instructions. Proverbs 8:33 says, ***"Listen to my instruction and be wise. Don't ignore it."*** There are a few believers who are not seeing or moving into the full manifestation of their Prophetic Promise or Prophetic Destiny. This is because they fail to take heed to the divine instructions given to them by their spiritual mentor or covering, the prophet or just a servant man or woman in ministry. God uses the gifts of the Spirit to prophetically announce your divine direction or instruction for their breakthrough, blessings or Destiny.

It was after the second miscarriage that God in His mercy reminded me of the word of knowledge received from the Late Deaconess Norman Hudson. I wept. When the Lord reminded me of the promise, I was on my knees seeking His face, repenting of desiring twins. I was recanting my desire to have twins because of the two failed pregnancies I had because in my mind and medical written and proven I couldn't handle or carry multiple babies in my womb to full-term. But little did I know that, the Lord had a greater plan, *'triple for my trouble'* and one more [Increase double, double]. What you can't do in your strength is made possible with His strength.

I beseeched the Lord to just give me just a man child. But shortly after I prayed that, He remined me of His promises that, *"He makes all things beautiful in His time and for my shame I shall possess the double."* The Lord used the miscarriages to refine me for greater. As you endure the refining process, the reflection of the Holy Spirit appears and becomes evident or visible in your life, business, or ministry as you totally submit to the process. Do you feel overtaken by afflictions, trials and the attacks of the enemy? Be reminded of Job, he worshipped while he waited on the Lord. I had to learn how to worship and wait on the Lord after the miscarriages.

Worship is evidence of brokenness. Your brokenness [evidence of repentance] is found in the fruit of your faith. Your brokenness before God shows evidence of your dependence on Him. Worship catapults you into the supernatural. Your worship Shifts the atmosphere for miracles and breakthroughs, that could not possible be attained in the natural surrounded by spiritual warfare and enemy forces. When you worship God during your season of afflictions it makes the process stress free because worship releases inner peace and outwardly creates an atmosphere for God to prophetically reset your life and annihilate the attack of the enemy.

Expectation is the Breathing Ground for Miracles

The promise is the breathing ground for expectation. The promise gives ground for expectation. Based on the binding agreement [covenant] God promises to fulfil His part, and you promise to walk in obedience to God's word and promise over your life. That promise gives you **"Divine Access"** and the right to expect that it will be completed. Declare it: *"My expectation is the breathing ground for my miracles."* I was confident that what the Lord spoke through Deaconess Norma Hudson in 2003 at the Women's Conference that God makes all things beautiful in its time will come to pass. But the journey to get there was filled with what seem like setbacks or roadblocks, hinderances and discouragements. But my late husband and I held on to the scriptures written on our bedroom door that we prayed daily: -

"Therefore, I tell you, all the things you pray and ask for--believe that you have received them, and you will have them [Mark 11:24]."

"Therefore, I tell you, all the things you pray and ask for--believe that you have received them, and you will have them." [Isaiah 53:5].

"Keep on asking, and you will receive what you ask for. Keep on seeking, and you will find. Keep on knocking, and the door will be opened to you" [Matt 7:7].

The Lord used my dark place to birth out what I can only describe as the **"Greatness of the Shift."** The birth of the triplet Abigail, Aaron, Nathaniel, then wo (2) later breakthrough contraceptive method of protection I had Joshua manifested after a I went through a dark place or period in my life, suffering two (2) miscarriages. During that difficult and painful moment, I was taking care of a husband who had several complications after an open-heart surgery. We were not even focus on getting pregnant because he spent over six (6) weeks laying in the hospital dealing with after effects of a surgery gone bad and clots were found in his portal vein. I remember clearly my mother came up to help from Jamaica that September 2005 while he was in the hospital.

It was in that season I got pregnant shortly after his recovery from that problem that was discovered after his surgery. So, I can testify to you that the season that seems like the worst period in your life as if a storm passed through that's when the Lord turn that thing around into a Mega Blessing. The Shift promised to you doesn't start on the mountain, it actually begins in the valley or in what I already describe as a dark place or period of transition in your life. Once the prophetic word is released, you must understand that it takes a process to get into your **"Greatness." "Greatness"** takes time. In my second book **"I Am Anointed for This,"** chapter 6 is entitled the **'Refiners Fire'** and it reveals that in your season of waiting, the Lord uses the afflictions you experience to refine you for **"Greatness,"** a new beginning or as we put it a **"Fresh Start."**

As I am writing this new book, I hear the Lord saying, *"you were almost there,"* and it seemed like someone or a spiritual attack came against your life to disrupt it. But the Lord is about to do a Prophetic Reset to restore you with double for your trouble, **"Mega-Blessings."** This happened to Joseph. This also happened to Daniel and the three (3) Hebrew boys. **"Prophetic Disruption"** shifted them from what appeared to be their place of comfort, into a valley experience to prepare them to experience the **"Greatness of the Shift"** for supernatural intervention, breakthroughs, deliverance and ultimately **"Mega Blessings."** This refining moment for them is what the Lord used to cultivate and build integrity and character in them.

It was during this place that seemed like a very dark place that they were forced to **"PUSH** [*Persevere, Until the Shift, Happens*], **Don't Abort Your Purpose Destiny Is Calling You"** into **"The Greatness of the Shift."** During the **"Shift"** or refining process God began to reveal His heart to Daniel. When you are going through your refining moment you have to keep your eyes focus on the Lord Jesus.

> ***"But Daniel was determined not to defile himself by eating the food and wine given to them by the king."***

Also, during Joseph **"Shift,"** what appeared to be a zealous young man with a dream, he was tested and proven in the Pit, Prison and then to the Palace. During these testing and trials, God began to stir up and develop spiritual maturity in Joseph. God will not release you into the fullness of your **"Mega Blessing,"** breakthrough or destiny until you are mature enough to handle it. Joseph's attitude brought him favor in the prison and then promotion to the palace. When people try to kill your dream or vision or do things to distract or take you off course, God use it as **"Prophetic Disruption"** to catapult you into the **"Greatness of the Shift"** for **"Mega Blessings."**

Chapter 11

From Barrenness into Greatness

The Lord used my dark place of multiple miscarriages to birth out triplets from my womb. That's what I call the **"The Greatness of the Shift"** into **"Mega Blessings."** From two (2) miscarriages to the miraculous birth of triplets. Yes, I said it right I had three (3) healthy babies born June 23, 2006. It was an exciting journey as I was told by the Lord to follow every instruction given by the doctors and it shall be well. Remember I told you that your **"Greatness of the Shift"** is marked by a Divine Instructions. I was instructed to eat triple serving as protein daily in each meal and drink one gallon of water daily to keep hydrated. I was also put in a place where I had to be on bed rest waiting patiently in prayer until my change manifest. It was the Divine Instruction given to me from the Lord to intensify my pursuit after Him through worship that God used to activate His promise in me. I was able to conceive and give birth through supernatural intervention by the Holy Spirit but with faith and obedience on my part the Suddenlies of God manifested in my life.

Based on medical history of one miscarriage previously and fibroids that my Obstetrician for the second pregnancy used my history as mockery, reminding me at every prenatal checkup what my natural circumstances were. But he failed to understand that my God can do *"exceedingly and abundantly far above all I can ask or think according to the power that worketh in us"* [me].

- Who would have thought with multiple fibroids I could conceive and give birth to triplets from my womb, then two (2) years later another child?
- Who would have thought it possible with the doom message of fibroids and constant UTI's this **"Supernatural Shift"** could manifest?

Not to mention, my doctors last words to me after I went for a follow up visit from the miscarriage was even if it's possible there is a slim chance he said. I told him I fasted and prayed for three [3] days before I met with him. I told him the God I serve is able, and I have faith to believe that he will fulfill what he promises to me. The doctor replied, *"well then, let me refer you to a genetics Doctor, they may be able to tell you why you keep losing your babies."* I later learned from that "Genetics Doctor" without getting my file information on my initial visit to him after the second miscarriage that fibroids did not kill my baby. It was the UTI and dehydration that was left untreated by my doctor that complicated my pregnancy not fibroids.

Let me encourage you, let me speak life to you. You are a prime candidate for the **"Greatness of the Shift"** encounter. Don't be disheartened or be feeling letdown, as if God has forgotten you, you are a candidate for a supernatural release and an uncommon miracle. God is preparing you to shift from nothing into something big and beautiful. God is preparing you and He's getting ready to shift you from ***"Barrenness into Greatness."***

Like I said, The Lord use my dark place to propel me to *Push Until Something Shift in Worship*, just like Hannah did. I obeyed the Lord and intensified my seek after Him as well as increased my level of worship. This activated the seeds within me spiritually first and then natural to conceive and give birth to four children by only two (2) pregnancies. Your promise is given to you as a seed. That's why the scripture says, **"Therefore I tell you, all the things you pray and ask for believe that you have received them, and you will have them"** [Mark 11:24]. This was one of the verses we prayed daily as husband and wife until the seed germinated.

> **"Therefore, I say unto you, What things soever ye desire, when ye pray, believe that ye receive them, and ye shall have them."**

Who would have thought it was possible with the doom message of fibroids, constant UTI, and my doctors last words to me after I went for a follow up visit from the miscarriage was even if it's possible there is a slim chance and you might have to be on bed rest. I told him I fasted and prayed for three (3) days before I met with Him. I told him the God I serve is able, and I have faith to believe He will fulfill what he promised to me. He said, *"well then, let me refer you to a genetics Doctor, they may be able to tell you why you keep losing your babies"*. May I add that, the doctor said it casually as if he did not believe I could, but I was confident as 1 John 4:4 declares: -

> ***"Ye are of God, little children, and have overcome them: because greater is he that is in you, than he that is in the world."***

The Lord spoke to me, as I shared in Chapter 6 of my second **book "I Am Anointed for This**," saying,

> *"Daughter, I know you love me and desire to worship me in Spirit and in truth." "I want you to constantly praise me, this will counter and defeat the attacks of the enemy against your life."*

He further stated that,

> *"The only way to conquer these attacks is through worship." "You have no other option than to praise your way through. I want you to praise me constantly every day,"* The Lord further clarified how to worship. He said, *Worship me with Psalm, hymn and spiritual song as well as worshipping in the spirit"* [Worshipping in tongues].

The Lord will always give you a strategy to conquer and win. One year later without the help of any fertility treatment as customary and is a common treatment for mostly Caucasian and some African American women in the United States I discovered I was pregnant with triplets. The genetics and fertility doctors had me do bi-weekly blood work and told us when it was peak time for us to be intimate and still didn't get pregnant. Even my late husband was tested and proven that he too was fertile. Remember, the only reason I was sent to the Genetics Doctor was to run test to see why I couldn't carry a baby to full-term. I say it like this: *"The only reason why I went to a Genetics Doctor is to prove the devil wrong."* I got frustrated with these blood work and stopped going for my regular visits. But I never stopped praying, **"men ought always to pray, and not to faint"** [Luke 18:1].

At my last appointment before I decided to give up on these tests the Junior Doctor was on duty because the Senior Doctor was on vacation. He gave me the blood work results as well as a brochure about fertility treatment and told me to speak to the Senior Doctor when he returns on my next visit. He gave me instructions to go home and discuss it with my husband. I shared with my husband the information I received from the doctor on duty. I magnified prior testimonies of others prayed for as a ministered to them who received their miracles of conception and giving birth to their children. I shared with my husband that, I've seen God do it for others I prayed for several times who could not have children and even was instructed to do surgeries and surgery were cancelled. He agreed that the God we serve is able and we were confident He would do it. We desired a testimony that was not artificially inseminated but supernaturally generated. I wanted to experience ***"The Greatness of the Shift."***

Anyway, when I went to see the Senior Doctor for my check up after his vacation, I told him what the Junior Doctor recommended to me. He was in shock. He was trying to hold back his anger, but I could see the frustration on his face with what the Junior Doctor suggested to me. He said I will not recommend that to you, there's no need for that. I told him I agree. I never went back like I said earlier. Two weeks after they didn't see me come in for my routine blood work, the Office Assistant called to say the Senior Doctor would like to see me. He said I know you feel like we can't help you anymore, but we have done all the test that proves, ***"it is well."*** He said what I want you to do is try and lose 25 pounds and come back to me in two months.

A month after my last visit I missed my monthly menstrual cycle and I called the doctor to let them know I need to come in. Long story short the blood work proved I was pregnant, and I didn't lose any weight as the doctor implied was necessary for me to get pregnant. I believe they felt their integrity was on the line because they were not able to help me. Therefore, they had to come up with other alternatives such as go lose 25 pounds. I was only weighting 150 pounds. The numbers from the blood work results of pregnancy test were extremely high. So, they asked me to come and see them in two weeks to do an ultrasound. I was so naïve I didn't know that the higher numbers meant there is a possibility of multiples until I got to the Doctor's Office to do the Ultrasound Exam.

It was obvious that they didn't expect me to get pregnant with triplet because of the multiple fibroid they were expecting to see one. The nurse ran from the room in less than two to three (2-3) minutes of examining the uterus externally with the gel on my belly, saying, *"I need the doctor, I'll be right back."* The Junior Doctor came in with the nurse. After careful viewing the ultra sound monitor, he started counting, 1,2.3... Then the nurse rebuts and said no 1.2... The Doctor insisted that his count was accurate and repeated 1,2,3...again. I was so nervous because the nurse never told me why she was leaving the room. I said Lord I can't take another disappointment, why are they counting. I hope and prayed in that moment it wasn't fibroids. I said, *"can you tell me what is really is going on, why are you counting."* They both echoed you are pregnant with triplet. The Doctor clarified, *"We three (3) babies inside"* and turned the monitor of the screen so I could view.

    He said return in two weeks for another ultrasound and we will see if there is still three (3) fetus' inside your womb. I was wondering going home why would he think it would be less. So, I went to do my own research and sure enough at times, one fetus can disappear or abort itself naturally. But that wasn't my case. When God is in the plan it is irreversible. The doctors out of concern upon my return for my second ultrasound realizing there were still three babies growing beautifully in my womb, they recommended seeing that specialist for high risk pregnancies to terminate one of the babies. He said based on my history with fibroids I should go home and think about it. The same doctor who gave me hope now suddenly got nervous and wavering that I would be at risk also not just the babies if I try to go forward with all of them growing inside of me. I listened to the voice of God and not fear.

> ***"For God hath not given us the spirit of fear; but of power, and of love, and of a sound mind"*** [2 Timothy 1:7].

I didn't follow up with the specialist they recommended. I fasted and prayed for three (3) days until noon and the Lord redirected me to an Obstetrician who has experience in caring for expectant Mothers carrying multiples. Under the care of Dr. Bonefield the Lord told me, *"just follow all the directives and instructions given to you by him and you will be fine because this pregnancy has nothing to do with you."*. The Lord told me, this pregnancy has nothing to do with you, I am in full control. Well, it seems while I was sitting and waiting in the presence of God like Hannah, the Lord stepped in. The Lord is about to step into your situation suddenly. I remained constant in worshipping at the Lord's feet.

I lived and breathed Hannah's story right through my journey and then when it felt like there was nothing left to pray in reference to

Hannah's story, I prayed, ***"give me children lest I die,"*** my husband touched and agreed with me, even though he panicked when I said ***"lest I die,"*** with a smile I said no honey, not literally but it's a cry of desperation. Every night during the year of the miscarriages until the miraculous conception of the triplet, we decreed and declared prophetically Mark 11:24 daily and two other scriptures verses every night, Isaiah 53:5 and Matthew 7:7. We anoint ourselves each time asking the Lord to bless our bodies and make it fruitful.

These scriptures are still present today posted on my room door. After such a long period of waiting and healing emotionally from the loss of my babies, the devil tried to put me in a trap to waiver at the promise. If I had waivered for a minute and tried to remove one of those fetuses the Lord revealed to me that all the babies would have died in the process. I am shouting, and singing right now, look what the Lord has done, **"The Greatness of the Shift"** experience into <u>an intriguing testimony of the miraculous birth of my triplet, Abigail, Aaron, Nathaniel and two (2) years later breaking the barriers of limitation Joshua Manning came forth.</u>

Again, let me remind you, don't let your suffering, or pain be an excuse to remain stagnant or immobile. Don't allow the ridicule, insults, jealousies or rejection from men become an hinderance to you stepping into greatness and leaping into your destiny. Get up and use these negative arrows against you to **"P.U.S.H, [*Persevere, Until the, Shift, Happen*], Don't Abort Your Purpose Destiny is Calling You."** It was a familiar ground for Jabez and it was also a familiar ground for Hannah, where every day they wake up expecting the same thing to happen, pain and ridicule. Constantly being reminded of their barrenness and pain by the way they were treated, but God turned their pain into praise.

- God turned their pain into power.
- God turned their pain into fruitfulness,
- God turned their pain into promotion.
- God turned their pain into enlargement of territory.
- God turned their story around from Barrenness into Greatness for a Mega Blessing.

Likewise, God turned my painful miscarriages experience that could have traumatized me to the point of losing my mind into power birthed through a divine instruction to intensify my praise. This experience was the breathing ground for my miracles. God not only turn my pain into power. He also turned my pain into fruitfulness, promotion and enlargement of territory. Since this journey and overcoming these obstacles, I have stood on global platforms ministering and praying for several women who received their healing and gave birth to their child, even one couple had twins now two (2) years old.

I want to encourage someone today that**, "Your Place of Pain, Shall Become Your Place of Praise."** God hears and understand your cry. Whether it is a cry for help or a cry of distress. It may be a cry or lament with words you cannot express he interprets them all. Sometimes we cry because we feel hurt or let down, he understands that too.

> *"The righteous cry, and the Lord heareth, and delivereth them out of all their troubles"*
> (Psalm 34:17).

> And *"When I cry unto thee, then shall mine enemies turn back: this I know; for God is for me"* (Psalm 56:9).

Read also Psalm 13. I pray you will be strengthened by the revelations, inspirations and my personal testimonies throughout this book. I pray that your healing and deliverance will come speedily in Jesus name amen.

Meet the Triplets at birth June

Meet Joshua as New Born

Chapter 12

Beware of Destiny Killers

Dream Killers or Destiny Killers are fueled by jealousy and hatred. Dream Killers or Destiny Killers see your hard work and effort paying off and refuse to pay the price. Destiny Killers can see that you possess greater on the inside of you. But they give an opposite reaction of being critical, contentious, mocking you, humiliating you or reject you to distract you from pursing or focusing on your promise.

If I had listened to the doctor's fear of me losing the triplet babies due to fibroids, I would not be testifying today of my four (4) bundles of joy. Brothers and sisters there are some folk who are only focus on your history they are called **"Destiny Killers." "Destiny Killers"** never ever give you any hope. **"Destiny Killers"** has no vision. I was blessed, that I had my late husband and best friend who gave me hope, and who was a man of vision. I was blessed to have him during this painful journey and loss. A man who walked in the power of the prophetic, the gift of Discerning of Spirits and he was also a strong intercessor. I still have a praying mother and a remnant of friends and confidants that still holds my children and myself up with encouragement, love and prayers. The bible says, **"Without a vision the people perish."**

- Destiny Killers hate you just because you are a dreamer.
- Destiny Killers hate you just because you are blessed.
- Destiny Killers or Dream Killers are intimidated by what they see in you as a promise, gift or talent.
- Destiny Killers remain negative because they have no vision for their own lives, just like Sanballat and Tobias.
- Destiny Killers are afraid of what they see in you.
- Destiny Killers are afraid of what God is doing through you.
- Destiny Killers are afraid or intimidated by what they see God is doing for you.

Don't Listen to Dream Killers

Be very careful who you open to about your dream or visions. God has a plan for your life. When God gives you, a sure word stand on it. Whatever the plan, purpose, blessings, healing or deliverance, He spoke or revealed to you through the Word of God concerning your destiny, **"BELIEVE."** Believe regardless of how you might feel about our life situations that you have experienced or about your situation even now. Believe regardless of what negative people say. To win the battles or spiritual warfare we face and encounter you must have **"NOW FAITH."** Your faith carries you through the storm. Always remember there is purpose in the storm.

> *"For I know the plans I have for you, says the Lord. They are plans for good and not for evil, to give you a future and a hope"* [Jeremiah 29:11].

Even though situations may remain the same, or possibly intensify. Understand that birthing is painful and whatever the Lord is about to birth out of you it is great. Check the record of Job, Daniel, David, Jacob, Moses and Joseph to name a few, these great men had storms, but it was all apart of a process and a plan for greater. The one thing the Lord requires of you is for you to seek Him and you will find Him when you search for Him with all your heart.

> ***"Then shall ye call upon me, and ye shall go and pray unto me, and I will hearken unto you. ¹³ And ye shall seek me, and find me, when ye shall search for me with all your heart. ¹⁴ And I will be found of you, saith the Lord: and I will turn away your captivity, and I will gather you from all the nations, and from all the places whither I have driven you, saith the Lord; and I will bring you again into the place whence I caused you to be carried away captive"*** [Jeremiah 29:12-14].

Someone we know very well celebrated after I had the second miscarriage. They called to tell me that Sunday morning how they had a dream about my baby and they knew my baby would have died. They were laughing on the phone as if it was great news to deliver to an already broken woman, who was discharged without a new born baby that, **"I knew it, I**

knew your baby was going to die, I dreamt it." Your dilemma or crisis will expose your worst enemies.

When God gives you a word of promise for blessings, healing, deliverance, miracle or breakthrough, hold on to it. Refuse to listen to **"Dream Killers."** Once God has declared the best is yet to come, you can expect someone coming along to speak gloom or doom over it! Satan beguiled Eve and thwart the initial plan of paradise in the Garden of Eden. Some people don't want to see you succeed, or they are just ignorant and insensitive. I said to her on the other end of the line, *"my God told you my baby was going to die, and you didn't pray for me?"* She went silent on the other end of the line, and then answered no. I hung up. She came by next day trying to reach me I was not led to and could not open the door, I was so distraught. I wept for over a week. I couldn't stop, even when I wanted to, tears just gushed out unexpectedly.

I forgave her and continue to hope and dream again. Even though Satan beguiled Eve and Adam and Eve was forbidden to remain in the Garden of Eden, nothing could stop God's plan of redemption for mankind. Through Jesus Christ the second Adam we have access to salvation. Nothing can hinder God's plan ad purpose., all things work for the greater good. The blood of Jesus was shed to bring us in connection to unlimited power and resources. Dream Killers may try to delay the plan of God, but they have no power to stop the plan. I want to pause to encourage you again, no matter what others say or do to discourage you mock you or become critical of your situation, **P.U.S.H. [*Pray, Until, the Shift, Happens*] "Don't Abort your Purpose Destiny is Calling You"** into **"The Greatness of the Shift."** You are **"Destined for Greatness,"** hence the reason why the fight, opposition, oppression and warfare are great.

Who Are You Eating With?

> *"For as he thinketh in his heart, so is he: Eat and drink, saith he to thee; but his heart is not with thee"*[Proverbs 23:7].

God will expose your haters, our Destiny hijackers and Destiny killers right before your very eye as they try to eat with you or entice you to eat with them. They are eating with you and trying to serve you the plate of grudge, jealousy and envy! Delilah seduced Samson to reveal His secrets to her knowing very well in her heart her intent was to weaken him to destroy him. Some draw near to you and tell you "You can trust me." But the moment you begin to open, and they discover the purity of your heart, kindness, tender hearted-ness, they assume you are Mr. or Mrs. Weakness!

> ***"Thou preparest a table before me in the presence of mine enemies: thou anointest my head with oil; my cup runneth over"*** [Psalm 23].

What you are about to give birth to will not be miscarried. I declare to you that, God is about to checkmate them and reverse the sabotage against your destiny right back to the Sabotore!

Genesis 50:20 ***"As for you, you meant evil against me, but God meant it for good in order to bring about this present result..."***

I shared with you earlier that I received Divine Instruction from the Lord in the second week after the miscarriage as instructed by the Holy Spirit to take my worship to another level. He said, ***"I know you are an intense worshipper, but I want you to increase your pursuit after me through worship."*** My late husband came home that night and he laid hand on me. He said **"Nads, God wants me to anoint you and break that spirit of weeping over your life and your emotions."** He said, after this day, there shall be a turnaround according to Isaiah 61:3,

> *"To appoint unto them that mourn in Zion, to give unto them beauty for ashes, the oil of joy for mourning, the garment of praise for the spirit of heaviness; that they might be called trees of righteousness, the planting of the Lord, that he might be glorified."*

God took us from **"Barrenness into Greatness."** From having no children to a quiver full of children. The Lord manifested **"The Greatness of the Shift"** in our lives because we remained faithful even under the pressures of ridicule, loss and disappointment. God will take you from **"Barrenness to Greatness."**

> *"Behold, children are a heritage from the Lord, the fruit of the womb a reward. ⁴ Like arrows in the hand of a warrior are the children of one's youth. ⁵ Blessed*

is the man who fills his quiver with them! He shall not be put to shame when he speaks with his enemies in the gate"
[Psalm 127:3-5].

Once you ask God the purpose for your life don't give room to doubt or doubters, believe God. I am a living miracle and testimony of that truth, believing God. Dream Killers see the opportunity you have the opportunity you have that they also received but never made use of it. Now, here they come trying to block I am a Carrier of the Shift and I am chosen by God to become a Kingdom Shifter to help others unlock the greatness within them and to tap into their untapped potential.

Nothing you go through will be wasted but instead, it will be invested for greatness. Now, the Lord is using my life experiences, testimony and the anointing upon my life cultivated through fiery trials to help people globally breakthrough and break free from difficult maters and circumstances in their lives.

Never waver at the promise of God over my life. Let me enlighten you what is about to happen. While the Destiny Killers are focus on your history, God shall use your story of hard-pressed trials, and suffering to create a greater history that will transforms lives. The latter rain in your life will be greater than the former rain. I feel a shout right here. Your history shall produce and bring God Glory. My history from the medical odds, evidence through miscarriage said impossible but God says, with Him ***"all things are possible."*** **"The Greatness of the Shift"** makes what seem impossible, made possible through Jesus Christ, all you need is mustard seed faith.

Chapter 13

The Glory is in Your Story

The miracles of Jesus were made manifest in and through our lives suddenly. We were featured on the front page of the Daily Journal Newspaper for Southern New Jersey in June 2006 as we shared our miraculous journey and birth of the triplet. The Lord will use your history to bring glory to His name. As a result of which the power, blessings, miracles and breakthrough you experience comes from the process you had to endure and overcome. Therefore, the glory is in your story.

> ***"But we have this treasure in earthen vessels, that the excellency of the power may be of God, and not of us"***
> [2 Corinthians 4:7].

The Obstetrician who mocked me and made fun of my situation lost his mind a year later to Dementia. He deceptively led me to a hospital that he was an hour away from. Not to mention, his Medial Practice was not even registered to visit patients there. He led me far and wide he felt that there was no hope for me and my baby. I could have driven to the hospital in the city where he was licensed to practiced but instead, he advised me to go home and lie down, put your legs up. How insensitive he was to my situation.

When I tell you Hannah's Story is my story, for God's Glory it was. There are some people who mock you like Peninnah mocked Hannah in 1 Samuel Chapter 1, but *"I speak life over you that you will not be put to shame, neither will you be confounded before your enemies."* Maybe you have a similar story of a doctor who mocked you and gave you no hope. You may be surrounded by those who claim they love you but are very deceptive. Let me remind you what Psalm 23 says, **"Thou preparest a table before me in the presence of my enemies."** God's promise is irrevocable and unstoppable. In 1997 it was already prophetically spoken over my life by the renown Prophet Andrew Scott, Pastor of Greater Works Ministry that I shall be a mother of Nations like Sarah. What the Lord confirmed through the mouth of the prophet was made manifest nine (9) years later.

Delay is not denial, it may seem long, months or even years. Bishop Norman Lewin reminded me recently that greatness takes time. When the Lord is working on your miraculous blessing, healing or breakthrough it may seem a dark and winding road. But to cultivate something big and beautiful it is in the details that is called the process into greatness. Go through your process patiently enduring through faith into the Prophetic Promise given to you. We endured the process by walking in obedience to the Lord's Divine Instructions given to us and we had four (4) children miraculously because of God's supernatural intervention in our lives.

The ***"Glory is in Your Story"*** means our destination into Destiny takes you into not only new dimensions in God, but it opens new doors that no man can shut as well as carries you into the new experiences of miracles, blessings and breakthrough. My paternal grandmother worked as a midwife in the United Kingdom [UK] until she retired and returned to Jamaica to live as a Pensioner. I believe the Lord set the tone for what my Destiny entails and the anointing I would carry through my paternal grandmother initially. My mother was like a daughter to her and they were very close. My mother is also a midwife spiritually as well, because she has mothered many sons and daughters. She travailed persistently until I gave my life to Christ.

My paternal grandmother is a pioneer because her journey for a better life in the United Kingdom prepared me years later for what I am doing as missionary work globally as lives are being impacted greatly. Through Apostle Dr. Nadine Manning Ministries Inc. lives are being impacted globally. Because of this story of my children's miraculous conception, God has spiritually placed within me the capacity and the anointing to become a **"Carrier of the Shift."** As an Apostolic Mid-Wife the Lord has equipped me to help men and women give birth to their purpose, dream and visions. The Lord not only used me in Jamaica to release men and women naturally and spiritually to give birth to their promise, purpose and ultimate destiny, but also in the United States and the United Kingdom [UK].

In September 2016 I was the guest speaker in the United Kingdom for a three (3) day Women's Conference where the Lord used me to pray for a renowned Bishop in the New Testament Church of God, daughter in law who was trying to conceive but was unsuccessful until the "Shift happened. When you are a Carrier of the Shift, the Suddenlies of God will be evident wherever you go. After praying for her, few months later I received an email she was with child. I gave her the same Divine Instructions the Lord gave me, it was to intensify her worship and seek after Him. That child is now eight to nine (8-9) months old baby boy.

The significance of this UK story is that my paternal grandmother was a midwife in the UK and I was the first her grandchildren to travel to the UK since she retired and resettled in Jamaica. Neither did any of her children ever visited the UK. My paternal grandmother was a **"Carrier of the Shift,"** and this anointing was supernaturally transferred to my **"DNA of Destiny"** with Royal Access to My Inheritance to not only conceive and give birth to multiples physically but also to spiritually help others experience **"The Greatness of the Shift"** I prophecy over you that:

> *"Those who mocked you shall sit at the table and watch your cup brim over with blessings," they shall watch the Shift Anointing Oil of Greatness be poured upon you. They shall stand by*

and watched the perpetual whirlwind of God's favor moving in your life.

When I had the second miscarriage, I took the advice of the nurse on duty that morning and held my still-born baby. She said it will help you after you leave this place. You must be willing to **'Break the Box'** and **'Be Ready to Shift.'** Learn from my own personal experience and testimony in this book, as well as my other books available on Amazon.com or through our ministry. As shared in my first published book **"Awake to Your Destiny"** that God released me to emerge out of a very dark and ugly period in my life when I suffered in silence to birth out my first book. Since then my life has been catapult into what I can only describe as the **"Greatness of the Shift."** Who would have thought that I would be able to produce and birth out triplets and yet still another child two (2) years later after my womb was condemned by a Peninnah spirit in the form of a Medical Doctor. You don't get to choose your test. Life without painful test or trials cannot birth out greatness.

When you have experienced **"the Greatness of the Shift,"** you are empowered as a **Kingdom Shifter**, to announce to others, as well to release a clarion sound prophetically that, **"Greater is Coming."** I lost two (2) babies by miscarriage but the Lord restored and multiplied what I lost into Greater. The birth of the triplets, Abigail, Aaron and Nathaniel made the Daily Journal Newspaper in 24 hours after their birth. Two years later, a had another son Joshua. What the Lord spoke to me as a Prophetic Promise manifested that *"for your [my] shame you [I] shall possess the double..."*

    I did everything to prevent having another child after the birth of the triplets using contraceptive methods. I still got pregnant, because when God announces double for your trouble that means from the two (2) miscarriages he would double what I lost. That means 2 x 2 = 4. There was nothing I could physically, medically or naturally do to prevent having a fourth (4th) child even if I tried because **"The Greatness of the Shift"** will breakthrough every barriers of limitations. **"The Greatness of the Shift"** is supernatural, **"The Greatness of the Shift"** it's a God thing, not a man thing.

    What can you take away from this Divinely Ordained book and my personal testimonies throughout?

- Stay in the game.
- Stay with your purpose.
- Stay longer than the world thinks you can, pushing and pursuing your passion.
- P.U.S.H. beyond the place or limits society has placed on you pursuing your dreams and visions.

> *"The winter solstice has always been special to me as a barren darkness that gives birth to a verdant future beyond imagination, a time of pain and withdrawal that produces something joyfully inconceivable, like a monarch butterfly masterfully extracting itself from the confines of its cocoon, bursting forth into unexpected glory"* [Gary Zukav].

Joel 2 declares that:

> **"And it shall come to pass afterward, that I will pour out my spirit upon all flesh; and your sons and your daughters shall prophesy, your old men shall dream dreams, your young men shall see visions: 9 And also upon the servants and upon the**

handmaids in those days will I pour out my spirit."

What is that burning fire or passion in your heart? That fire is your message. That fire has your blessing or breakthrough in it. That fire is your dream or vision. That fire is your cellular DNA of Destiny telling you that you have the opportunity or responsibility to accomplish it or birth it out and this is where Kingdom Shifters are made. **P.U.S.H. [Persevere, Until, the Shift, Happens] "Don't Abort Your Purpose Destiny is Calling You into "The Greatness of the Shift."**

> *I decree and declare that your future beyond imagination, I decree and declare that your time of pain and withdrawal shall produces something joyfully inconceivable, like a monarch butterfly masterfully extracting itself*

from the confines of its cocoon, bursting forth into unexpected glory." I prophecy and release through these pages the unleashing of the unexpected glory and the Suddenlies of God in your life in Jesus name, Amen.

A Witness Testify to the Prophetic Word I was given

Andrea Burke's testimony of her witnessing me receiving the prophecy from Prophetess Miller concerning having multiple children.

> *"You had to give birth to more than one baby Apostle. I remember a prophecy you received many years ago, at the Holy Childhood Auditorium in Kingston, I don't know if you remember. It was husband and wife Prophet and Prophetess. You and I were sitting in the front row, the Prophetess took you from your seat, she warned that what the Lord told her to do will appear strange us, and she allowed you to lay on your back, and she prophesied and imparted the anointing that was on her to you. Then she told you, she saw triplets.*
>
> *Apostle Nadine, you were called, you have walked, lived, impacted and imparted what's in you. I'm a*

testimony. You are going global in Jesus name. Through your radical anointing I am who I am today. You taught me to pray and worship. All those late nights coming from street meetings supporting you carrying my babies each night along with me, who have become wonderful young men today. Apostle Manning you're blessed."

To my fellow readers **"Don't Abort Your Purpose Destiny is Calling You into the Greatness of the Shift."** Doctor's told me to choose between abortion or the risk of miscarriage instead I choose **LIFE** and gave birth to Triplet, (Abigail, Aaron and Nathaniel) and then two (2) years later another Divine Miracle (Joshua).

There's Greatness in You.
"THE GREATNESS OF THE SHIFT" book with my testimony of the Miraculous birth of my children will transfigure you into the Supernatural Realm to untap your potential and **Leap into Your Destiny - Walking into GREATNESS.**

Contact Us @

- Apostlenadineglobal@gmail.com
- Tel. 609-972-6346
- Instagram – Drnadine_globalshiftnetwork
- Facebook – Apostle Nadine Manning Global Ministries, Nadine H. Manning Global Shift Network

Mailing Address:

P.O. Box 91
Millville, New Jersey, 08332

Website:

www.apostlenadineglobal.com

Apostle Dr. Nadine Manning Books available for purchase @

- www.amazon.com

- or www.apostlenadineglobal.com

Book Titles

- Awake to Your Destiny
- I Am Anointed for This
- I Am Anointed for this Prophetic Unlocking

- The Prophetic Unlocking Intercessors Devotional
- Don't Abort Your Purpose – Destiny is Calling You into the Greatness of the Shift

www.ingramcontent.com/pod-product-compliance
Lightning Source LLC
Chambersburg PA
CBHW030855170426
43193CB00009BA/614